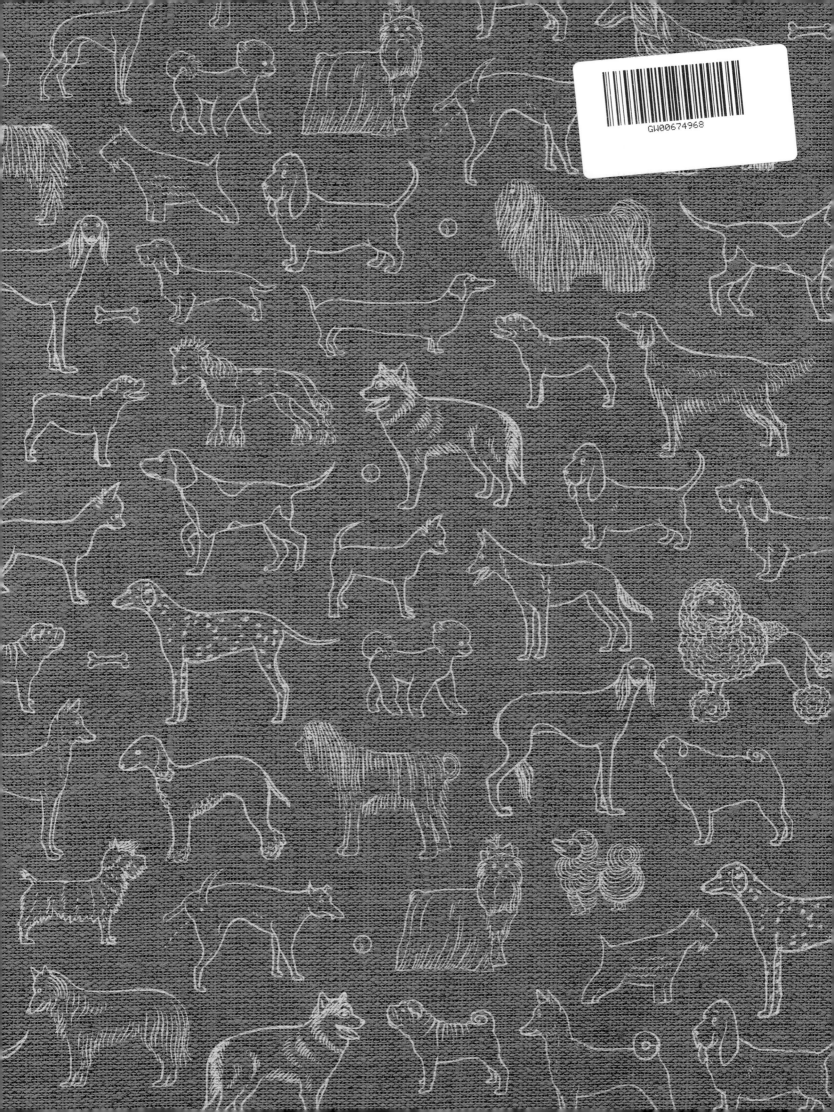

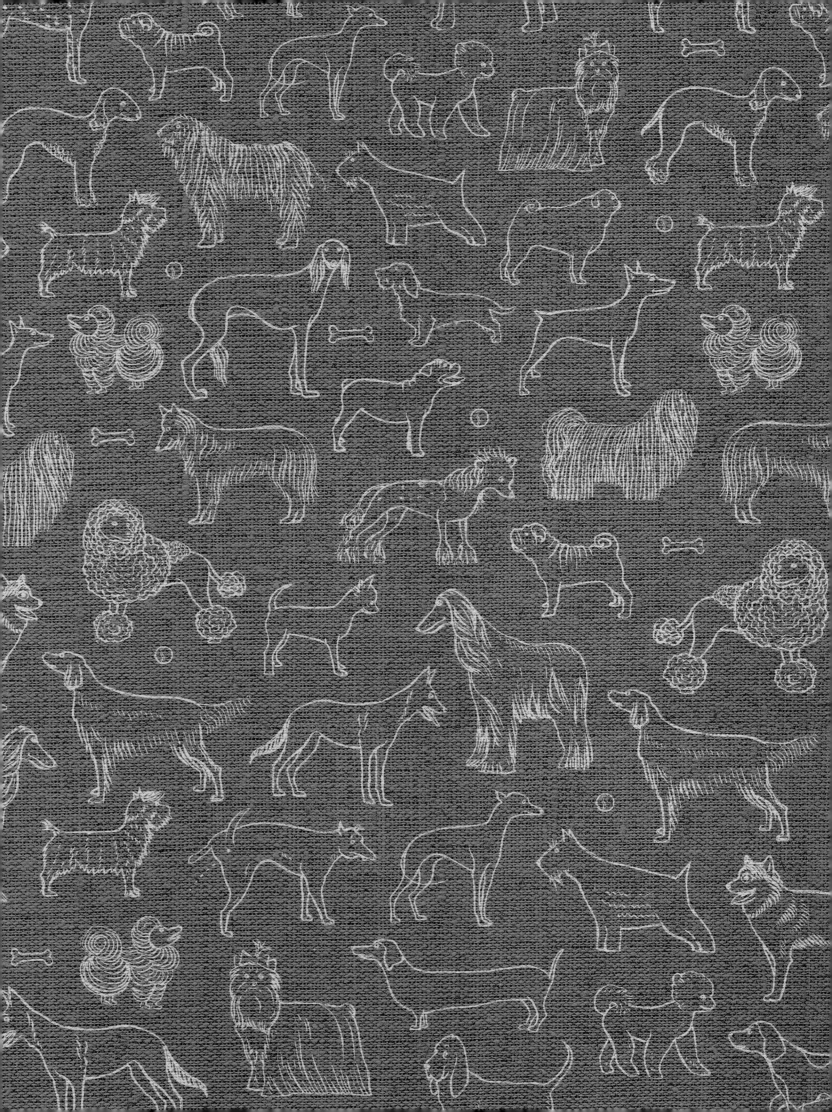

WINE DOGS

Australia

5

WINE DOGS

Australia

A PICTORIAL CELEBRATION OF CANINES
FROM THE GREAT WINE ESTATES OF AUSTRALIA

BY CRAIG McGILL AND SUSAN ELLIOTT

GIANT DOG

WINE DOGS

Australia

5

A PICTORIAL CELEBRATION OF CANINES
FROM THE GREAT WINE ESTATES OF AUSTRALIA

BY CRAIG McGILL AND SUSAN ELLIOTT

GIANT DOG

BILLIE FOUR-MONTH-OLD NOVA SCOTIA DUCK TOLLING RETRIEVER, ARTWINE, WOODSIDE, SA

FOREWORD

by Michael Leunig

GROWING AND MAKING WINE is an ancient undertaking fraught with calamities, disappointments and mysteries galore. Things go wrong, necessities fail, and nature becomes petulant and uncooperative. Winegrowers stumble about in frustration, uttering the language of rural despair. They curse their fate; they wring their hands, they shake their fists at the sky. And this is precisely where wine dogs come in.

As we all understand, dogs are the most skillful psychotherapists known to humankind. When nobody else cares or understands, a dog casually appears out of nowhere, and in two shakes of a sympathetic tail, brings vital perspective and sets things right. As skillful counsellors, as compassionate consolers, as wise court jesters, their healing work is famous and undisputed.

Their soulful depth is as precious in the vineyard as it is in the shed or the cellar – or anywhere around the house for that matter. In fact the term 'working dog' refers mainly to the fact that dogs are miracle workers.

Of course, not all of these miracles are benevolent or helpful to the owner, as various biographical notes about certain dogs in this book will verify. How a pooch can manage to open a fridge door and snaffle three kilograms of pork sausages destined for a birthday barbecue is indeed a miracle. How it managed to eat all of the sausages in just a few minutes, including the paper they were wrapped in, is indeed a miracle within a miracle.

Interestingly, although the wine dog usually has a frightful weakness for sausages and kleptomania, it does not normally drink wine, and this is simply because it does not need to. The reason dogs have no need for wine is simply because they have tails to wag.

This is the same reason why they do not make art. The tail is truly an amazing piece of equipment. If humans had tails to wag they would also not need to drink wine or make art. Gambling, playing chess or golf, compulsive interior decoration, riding vintage motor bikes or dancing the tango; all these sorts of activities would be unthinkable and unnecessary if we had tails to wag. What a pity.

This brings us to the delicate subject of human shortcomings. Even the briefest glance into a newspaper or television screen these days will probably confirm to us that humanity is not doing very well just lately, and in many cases is behaving quite dismally.

A glass of wine with the evening meal can be helpful in easing the disappointment about one's fellow creatures, and it may ease the discomfort that comes from being constantly exposed to so many photographs of crazed politicians, celebrities and models that are forced on us each day in the media, or gigantically emblazoned on buses and billboards wherever we go.

Oh those weird, anxious, desperate public faces of humankind. And even a trip on an overpopulated suburban train may leave our minds overloaded with strange faces that are not overly friendly. How we tire of them, and how we long for the sight of a natural face that is not devious or pained, not forced or false, but is innocent and good natured... That looks intelligent and sincere; that looks sweetly open and wise.

This is where books about wine dogs come in.

Reader, I ask you; look at the array of faces portrayed in this book... And what is this book if not a colourful gallery of vibrant portraits; interesting radiant faces that smile eagerly from the pages.

Unique faces of dogs depicting enormous intelligence and wellbeing. Faces that have lived. Faces of contentment. Alert unpretentious faces making a go of life and doing their best. Humble loveable faces full of honesty and character. Spirited faces.

Cheeky soulful smiles in abundance. Is this not heartening to behold? Is this not an effective simple antidote to world-weariness after another worrisome day on a troubled planet?

Readers, wine and dog appreciators... settle back in a cosy chair with these beautiful portraits of these glorious creatures. Contemplate their vitality and grace; their sheer dignity, then meditate upon your inner pooch and the joy therein. What a blessed relief it is.

Seeing as all of these wine dogs are listed as having owners, I think a small philosophical question about dog ownership is now appropriate.

Can anyone really own a dog? The idea seems strange somehow, just like the idea of owning one's children or spouse sounds all wrong. I think we might legitimately say we are the dog's chief benefactor, best friend or personal assistant; but owner...?

Hmmm, it seems to me that the wine dogs in this book are pretty much their own people; easy-going, charismatic, mostly cooperative, and amiable conversationalists for sure, but not entirely ownable. Isn't that one of the qualities we love about these fabulous dogs? Surely they are free spirits and all of them such unique individuals.

And finally, a note for the more pragmatic readers who need lots of useful hard information that will solve problems.

The task of naming a new pup can be one such problem; it can be a drawn-out and difficult consideration. Quite mind-bending actually. Many glasses of wine may be required. But worry no more, for here in these pages the problem is solved, and you will discover that this volume also amounts to a catalogue of marvellous dog names, all of great distinction.

Just go slowly back and forth through the book and choose a dog's face you are especially attracted to (the dog that is obviously falling in love with you) – and at the bottom of that page you will find its name – and of course this will be the perfect name for the beautiful amazing new pooch.

Cheers,
Michael Leunig

MICHAEL LEUNIG IS AN AUSTRALIAN CARTOONIST, WRITER, PAINTER, PHILOSOPHER AND POET. HIS COMMENTARY ON POLITICAL, CULTURAL AND EMOTIONAL LIFE SPANS MORE THAN FIFTY YEARS AND HAS OFTEN EXPLORED THE IDEA OF AN INNOCENT AND SACRED PERSONAL WORLD. THE FRAGILE ECOSYSTEM OF HUMAN NATURE AND ITS RELATIONSHIP TO THE WIDER NATURAL WORLD IS A RELATED AND RECURRENT THEME. HIS NEWSPAPER WORK APPEARS REGULARLY IN *THE MELBOURNE AGE* AND *THE SYDNEY MORNING HERALD*. HE DESCRIBES HIS APPROACH AS REGRESSIVE, HUMOROUS, MESSY, MYSTICAL, PRIMAL AND VAUDEVILLIAN — PRODUCING WORK WHICH IS OPEN TO MANY INTERPRETATIONS AND HAS BEEN WIDELY ADAPTED IN EDUCATION, MUSIC, THEATRE, PSYCHOTHERAPY AND SPIRITUAL LIFE. SINCE CHILDHOOD HE HAS BEEN A CLOSE FRIEND OF MANY FINE DOGS, HAS ENJOYED MANY GOOD BOTTLES AND HAS MADE SEVERAL BATCHES OF DELICIOUS RED WINE; HIS MOST MEMORABLE BEING A WONDERFUL GRENACHE IN THE LATE 1970s, THE BULK OF WHICH DISAPPEARED DURING A VERY LARGE AND LIVELY PARTY AT HIS PARENTS' HOME IN DAYLESFORD, VICTORIA.

The Wine Regions of our House.

Most of the truly great wines have been produced from the <u>pantry</u>, which is a cool climate region.

The fridge produces mainly white wines and the quality is mostly quite O.K.

Very drinkable wines have been produced from under the front seat of the car.

The shed is a warmer region but consistently produces some wonderful surprises.

A high-altitude region is the top of the bookshelf and perfectly magnificent wines can be found there. The letter box also produces the odd excellent bottle.

These days, wines are being produced from all sorts of unlikely and improbable places. Modern life is certainly creating some fascinating surprises.

HORACE

OWNER: MARY HAMILTON
FAVOURITE FOOD: RAW EGGS
OBSESSIONS: MARY AND FOOD
NAUGHTIEST DEED: TICKING OFF TO PRIMO
ESTATE FOR $60 PER KILO GRANA PADANO
FAVOURITE PASTIME: RIDING SHOTGUN IN CARS
FAVOURITE TOY: HIS COJONES (OOPS HE DOESN'T HAVE ANY)
PET HATE: BEING IGNORED – "I AM A HUMAN DOG YOU KNOW"

OBSESSION: JEREMY
PET HATE: BEING ALONE
FAVOURITE TOY: SQUEAKY PIG
FAVOURITE FOOD: CHICKEN BALLS
OWNERS: JEREMY AND DANIELA GORDON
FAVOURITE PASTIMES: CHEWING, SLEEPING
AND PLAYING WITH JACK AND TOM
NAUGHTIEST DEED: DAMAGING THE DINING ROOM FURNITURE

RALPH

MOLLY

PET HATE: CHEFS
OWNER: NICK BROWN
FAVOURITE TOY: TENNIS BALL
OBSESSIONS: CATS AND BIRDS
NAUGHTIEST DEED: STALKING THE DUCKS ON THE POND
FAVOURITE PASTIME: BEING ON THE BACK OF THE FORKLIFT

OWNER: ELIZA BROWN
PET HATE: SLEEPING OUTSIDE
FAVOURITE TOY: LARGE MIRROR
NAUGHTIEST DEED: SECRET POOS
OBSESSION: HIS OWN REFLECTION
FAVOURITE FOOD: MEDIUM-RARE STEAK

BARNABY

MERLOT

OWNERS: MARK AND MANDY CREED
OBSESSIONS: SMOKO AND HAPPY HOUR
FAVOURITE FOODS: WEDDING FARE, HIGH
TEA AND THE CHEF'S RECOMMENDATION
PET HATES: POSSUMS AND MISSING OUT ON FOOD
FAVOURITE TOYS: CAR SEATS (ANYTHING SOFT AND COMFY)
FAVOURITE PASTIME: SITTING AND LYING ON PEOPLE FOR LOVE
NAUGHTIEST DEED: DINING IN THE RESTAURANT AND GUESTS' ROOMS

MONTE

OWNERS: MARK AND MANDY CREED
NAUGHTIEST DEED: ATTACKING BIKES
PET HATES: BEING ALONE AND BIKE RIDERS
FAVOURITE PASTIME: TALKING TO HIS FAVOURITE PEOPLE
OBSESSIONS: GRANDMA, SWIMMING AND ROUNDING UP
FAVOURITE TOYS: MANNY'S EARS AND GRANDMA'S CHAIR
FAVOURITE FOODS: CORNFLAKES AND MONTE CARLO BISCUITS

FAVOURITE TOYS: BALLS AND STICKS
FAVOURITE PASTIMES: MEET N' GREET
AND SWIMMING IN THE DAM
OWNERS: LORETTA AND ANDY THOMPSON
OBSESSIONS: BALLS, FOOD, COUCH AND CUDDLES
NAUGHTIEST DEED: DESTROYING TWO PERSIAN RUGS, CARPET,
A FOUR-POSTER BED, AND A BEDSPREAD IN A TEETHING FRENZY

ARCHIE

LOTTE

OBSESSION: RIDING IN THE CAR

OWNERS: STEPHEN AND PRUE HENSCHKE

NAUGHTIEST DEED: EATING FALLEN GRAPES
ON THE WINERY FLOOR DURING VINTAGE

FAVOURITE TOY: A HOST OF FURRY ANIMALS
(WITH THE STUFFING FALLING OUT)

FAVOURITE PASTIME: SUNBAKING ON THE
WARM STONES IN FRONT OF CELLAR DOOR

FAVOURITE FOOD: A BONE OFFERED AS A DISTRACTION
FOR WHENEVER PRUE LEAVES THE PROPERTY

OBSESSION: FRISBEE
PET HATE: KANGAROOS
FAVOURITE TOY: FRISBEE
OWNERS: DUANE AND TANYA ROY
FAVOURITE FOOD: CHICKEN NECKS
FAVOURITE PASTIME: PLAYING FRISBEE
NAUGHTIEST DEED: EATING OUT OF A CUSTOMER'S
HANDBAG WHILE THEY WERE DOING A TASTING

NUTMEG

ROZIE

OWNER: MANDY JONES
PET HATE: OBEYING ORDERS
FAVOURITE TOY: HER BEDDING
FAVOURITE FOOD: ANYTHING THAT DROPS
ONTO THE FLOOR IN JONES WINERY RESTAURANT
NAUGHTIEST DEED: CHEWING PLANTS IN THE GARDEN

OBSESSION: FEET
OWNER: MANDY JONES
NAUGHTIEST DEED: CHASING THE CAT
FAVOURITE FOOD: GROTTY OLD BONES
PET HATES: HI-VIZ SHIRTS AND WORKBOOTS
FAVOURITE PASTIME: SCARING ANYONE WHO COMES INTO HER YARD

OBSESSION: THE DREGS FROM AMBER ALE
PET HATE: PEOPLE WHO DON'T ACKNOWLEDGE HIM
OWNERS: ADAM FIEGERT AND CHARLOTTE WILLIAMS
FAVOURITE PASTIME: SLEEPING IN THE SUN WHEN IT'S
COLD AND FINDING SOMEWHERE COOL WHEN IT'S HOT
NAUGHTIEST DEEDS: EATING GRAPES AND SLOBBERING
FAVOURITE FOOD: CHEESE KRANSKY FROM TANUNDA BAKERY
FAVOURITE TOY: BALLS FROM THE TENNIS COURTS NEXT DOOR

MOOSE

DAISY

FAVOURITE PASTIME:
SLEEPING IN FRONT OF THE FIRE
OWNER: TWO HANDS WINES
OBSESSIONS: CHASING RABBITS
AND CATCHING SOME RAYS
FAVOURITE FOOD: TURKEY NECKS
NAUGHTIEST DEED: RAIDING THE BINS

OWNER: TWO HANDS WINES
FAVOURITE FOOD: TURKEY NECKS
NAUGHTIEST DEED: JUMPING THROUGH
THE TOILET WINDOW TO JOIN GUESTS
FAVOURITE PASTIME: CHASING RABBITS
OBSESSION: SLEEPING IN THE GARDEN BEDS

SAFFY

LOUIS

OWNERS: CHRIS MOLINEAUX AND CLAIRE PORTER
PET HATE: THE DISCS ON THE MID-ROW CULTIVATOR
NAUGHTIEST DEED: ROLLING IN PILES OF COMPOST
FAVOURITE PASTIMES: RIDING UP THE FRONT OF THE
UTE AND RUNNING AROUND THE FARM WITH CLAIRE
OBSESSIONS: THE GARDEN RAKE AND THE OFFICE LADIES
FAVOURITE FOODS: MACARONI BALLS AND CHICKEN NECKS
FAVOURITE TOY: A FLUFFY, SQUEAKY SHEEP CALLED RAMMY

RAFFA

OBSESSION: THE SOCCER BALL
FAVOURITE PASTIME: PLAYING SOCCER
OWNERS: BRETT SMITH AND KRISTY GUIDERA
NAUGHTIEST DEED: PRUNING THE CHILLI PLANTS
FAVOURITE FOODS: CHICKEN NECKS AND CHEESE
PET HATES: MOTORBIKES, TRUCKS AND BROCCOLI
FAVOURITE TOY: JK THE SQUEAKY WEST COAST EAGLE

BAXTER

PET HATE: THE HOSE
FAVOURITE TOY: SONNY
OWNER: ALLANDALE WINERY
FAVOURITE FOOD: UNATTENDED LUNCHES
NAUGHTIEST DEED: KILLING THE PET CHICKENS
FAVOURITE PASTIME: SCRATCHING THE DOOR TO COME IN.
THEN SCRATCHING THE DOOR TO GO OUT.
THEN SCRATCHING THE DOOR TO COME IN...
OBSESSIONS: FOOD AND SCARING PEOPLE IN HI-VIZ VESTS

OWNER: ANNA SNEDDON
FAVOURITE TOY: KANGAROOS
FAVOURITE PASTIME: HUNTING RABBITS
WITH BAXTER IN THE AFTERNOON
OBSESSION: TO BE AS PRETTY AS BAXTER
NAUGHTIEST DEED: EATING CELLAR DOOR
STAFF LUNCHES WHEN THEY AREN'T LOOKING
FAVOURITE FOODS: LAMB CUTLETS AND LEFTOVERS
PET HATE: BAXTER GETTING MORE COMPLIMENTS THAN HIM

SONNY

ALLANDALE WINERY LOVEDALE, NSW | RHODESIAN RIDGEBACK X, 3 & STAFFORDSHIRE BULL TERRIER X, 2

OWNER: LUCAS GRIGSBY
FAVOURITE TOY: TENNIS BALL
PET HATE: GETTING SPRAYED WITH WATER
NAUGHTIEST DEED: MARKING HIS TERRITORY
ON THE VINEYARD SUPERVISOR'S LEG
FAVOURITE FOODS: RABBIT LIVER AND KIDNEY
FAVOURITE PASTIME: RIDING IN THE BACK OF THE UTE
OBSESSION: CHASING FOLIAGE WIRES WHEN SHAKEN

JASPER

HONEYJUMBLES

PET HATE: RUNNING
FAVOURITE FOOD: PASTA
OWNERS: KEITH AND AMANDA TULLOCH
OBSESSION: SLEEPING UNDER THE DESK
FAVOURITE PASTIME: TRYING TO TALK LIKE A PERSON
FAVOURITE TOYS: TEDDY BEARS (TO CHEW) AND LULU'S EAR

PET HATE: STAYING HOME
OWNERS: KEITH AND AMANDA TULLOCH
FAVOURITE PASTIME: ROUNDING UP PEOPLE
OBSESSION: BEING WITH KEITH AT ALL TIMES
NAUGHTIEST DEED: CHEWING CANE FURNITURE
FAVOURITE TOY: THE WATER FROM WINERY HOSES
FAVOURITE FOODS: BACON AND PASTA WITH RAW EGG

LULU

LILLY BELLE

OWNERS: ROD AND SANDRA KEMPE
FAVOURITE PASTIMES: EATING, MEETING
PEOPLE AND ROLLING IN ANYTHING THAT SMELLS
FAVOURITE FOODS: CHICKEN, BACON AND APPLES
NAUGHTIEST DEED: THE MYSTERIOUS CHICKEN INCIDENT OF 2006
PET HATES: THUNDERSTORMS, THE POSTIE AND ANYONE WEARING HI-VIZ

OWNERS: THE PRIOR FAMILY
FAVOURITE FOOD: JAM TOAST FOR BREKKIE
FAVOURITE PASTIME: WAITING FOR LUNCHTIME
IN THE WORK SHEDS AND EATING ALL THE SCRAPS
FAVOURITE TOYS: BALL, STICK AND TUG-O-WAR ROPE
PET HATES: THUNDER, SCARE GUNS AND FIREWORKS
OBSESSION: STEALING AND CHEWING UP WORKERS' GLOVES
NAUGHTIEST DEED: HIDING FROM DAN WHEN IT'S TIME TO GO HOME

BUDDHA

FAVOURITE TOY: SQUEAKY CHICKEN
OBSESSION: HOPPING IN VISITORS' CARS
WHEN THEY ARE LEAVING CELLAR DOOR
PET HATES: MAGPIES ON HER LAWN AND THE WIND
FAVOURITE PASTIME: WAITING UNDER THE SMOKO
TABLE TO BE FED BITS OF APPLE BY THE CELLARHANDS
OWNERS: SARA, ARCHIE, RUPERT AND DIGBY FLETCHER
FAVOURITE FOODS: ROAST CHICKEN AND KANGAROO POO

ELSIE

PENLEY

OWNERS: THE TILBY FAMILY
NAUGHTIEST DEED: CHASING CARS
FAVOURITE FOODS: ROAST LAMB AND BONES
PET HATE: BEING AWAY FROM FOOD AND THE FAMILY
FAVOURITE TOY: STUFFED GREEN MOUSE USED TO TORMENT DAISY
FAVOURITE PASTIMES: CHASING DAISY THE KITTEN AND DIGGING HOLES
OBSESSION: SLEEPING ON MATT'S OR BRIDGE'S LEGS AT THE END OF THE BED

WILLOW

DIRK DIGGLER

OBSESSION: FOOD
PET HATE: TRADIES
OWNER: IAIN RIGGS
FAVOURITE FOOD: CHICKEN NECKS
*FAVOURITE PASTIMES: EATING, SLEEPING
AND ANNOYING BULA THE KELPIE*
NAUGHTIEST DEED: BITING IAIN'S BEST FRIENDS

From left:

TUX OWNERS: MIKE CREDARO AND NAANDI SKINNER
NAUGHTIEST DEEDS: DIGGING HOLES FOR HIS BONES
AND RIPPING UP TUPPERWARE CONTAINERS
FAVOURITE FOOD: ANYTHING BUT DOG BISCUITS
FAVOURITE PASTIME: SPENDING TIME AT THE BEACH

HARLEY OWNERS: CHRIS AND NICOLE CREDARO
PET HATE: GETTING WASHED AFTER GOING TO THE BEACH
OBSESSION: ALFRED THE GOOSE
NAUGHTIEST DEED: STEALING CLOTHES FROM THE
CLOTHES BASKET THEN MAKING EVERYONE CHASE HIM

MAX OWNERS: ROBERT AND PHYLLIS CREDARO
FAVOURITE FOOD: SPAGHETTI
FAVOURITE PASTIME: CHASING AND ROUNDING UP SHEEP
FAVOURITE TOY: THE FOOTY

JACK OWNERS: ROBERT AND PHYLLIS CREDARO
FAVOURITE FOOD: LASAGNE
OBSESSION: RIDING IN THE FRONT SEAT OF THE UTE
NAUGHTIEST DEED: SITTING ON THE LOUNGE AT NIGHT

From left:

DIGBY OWNERS: CHESTER OSBORN AND KATH TIDEMANN
FAVOURITE PASTIME: CHASING KANGAROOS
NAUGHTIEST DEED: DESTROYING AND EATING
A KID'S BIRTHDAY PARTY SPREAD
OBSESSION: SMOOCHING

OOPY OWNERS: CHESTER OSBORN AND KATH TIDEMANN
OBSESSION: BREAKING AND ENTERING THE CHICKEN COOP
NAUGHTIEST DEED: EATING THE TV REMOTE
FAVOURITE PASTIME: RAIDING BEDROOMS
FAVOURITE FOOD: CHOOK POO

OBSESSION: CUDDLES
PET HATE: LOUD NOISES
FAVOURITE TOY: BUGS BUNNY
NAUGHTIEST DEED: NIPPING ANKLES
OWNERS: JAMES AND CAREENA KELLIE
FAVOURITE PASTIME: PLAYING WITH GERTIE

FAVOURITE FOOD: CHICKEN
OBSESSION: SQUEAKY TOYS
FAVOURITE TOY: ANYTHING SQUEAKY
OWNERS: JAMES AND CAREENA KELLIE
FAVOURITE PASTIME: PLAYING WITH CHARLIE
PET HATE: ANYONE GETTING ATTENTION FROM JAMES
NAUGHTIEST DEED: PUSHING CHARLIE OUT OF THE WAY

OBSESSION: LEMONS
OWNER: OLIVER KELLIE
FAVOURITE TOY: LEMONS
FAVOURITE FOOD: CHICKEN
PET HATE: BEING WOKEN UP
FAVOURITE PASTIME: RUNNING
NAUGHTIEST DEED: GETTING INTO
THE BED IN THE MIDDLE OF THE NIGHT

ROSIE

REG

OWNER: JOHN RYMILL
OBSESSION: JOHN RYMILL
PET HATES: LIGHTNING, THUNDER AND BEING
TOLD WHAT TO DO BY PEOPLE OTHER THAN JOHN
FAVOURITE PASTIME: ROAD TRIPPING ON THE BACK OF
THE UTE – PREFERABLY OFF ROAD, BUT ANYWHERE IS FINE
FAVOURITE FOOD: CUPCAKES (SHARED WITH SMALL
CHILDREN) OR FRESH RABBIT PROVIDED BY PETER RYMILL

PET HATE: BOATING
NAUGHTIEST DEED: CRAPPING IN THE BOAT
OWNERS: JOHN RYMILL AND MARY HARVEY
FAVOURITE FOOD: UNDER DEVELOPMENT;
CURRENTLY FOND OF HORSE POO, BUT
TRYING TO WEAN HIM ONTO FRESH RABBIT
OBSESSION: CHASING ANYTHING THROWN BY THE HUMANS
FAVOURITE TOY: STUFFED RABBIT (NOW DECEASED, POSITION VACANT)
FAVOURITE PASTIME: FISHING IN THE RYMILL CELLAR DOOR GOLDFISH POND

MERV

FAVOURITE TOY: HIS LEAD
PET HATE: BEING LEFT BEHIND
FAVOURITE PASTIMES: WALKING AND
EATING (NOT NECESSARILY IN THAT ORDER)
OBSESSION: HIS GRANDFATHERS ON BOTH SIDES
NAUGHTIEST DEED: BARGING THROUGH THE DOOR
KNOWN ACCOMPLICES: THOMAS, GEORGE AND ELLIOT
OWNERS: SHAVAUGHN WELLS AND RANDALL CUMMINS

DUTTON

BILLIE

OWNERS: JUDY AND GLEN KELLY
FAVOURITE TOY: SQUEAKY DUCK
NAUGHTIEST DEED: EATING AN ENTIRE
CORNER OF A LOVELY AND EXPENSIVE RUG
PET HATE: BEING SEPARATED FROM COCO AND JUDY
OBSESSIONS: COCO, JUDY AND ANYTHING CHEWABLE
FAVOURITE PASTIME: JUMPING ON COCO AND PULLING HIS EARS

COCO

OBSESSION: JUDY
OWNERS: JUDY AND GLEN KELLY
FAVOURITE TOY: KONG STUFFED WITH TREATS
PET HATES: STORMS AND WINDSCREEN WIPERS
FAVOURITE FOODS: CHEESE AND PEANUT BUTTER
NAUGHTIEST DEED: STEALING FROM GUESTS' HANDBAGS
FAVOURITE PASTIMES: WATCHING TV AND BEING ANYWHERE JUDY IS

CASS

OWNER: PETER ALLEN
FAVOURITE FOOD: CHICKEN WINGS
FAVOURITE TOY: PLASTIC GARDEN POTS
FAVOURITE PASTIME: RIDING THROUGH
THE VINEYARD ON THE QUAD BIKE
PET HATE: PEOPLE TOUCHING HER PAWS
OBSESSIONS: SWIMMING AND GAS GUNS

MYRTLE

OWNER: MELANIE CHESTER
OBSESSIONS: BATS (IN A BAD WAY)
AND TRADESMEN (IN A GOOD WAY)
FAVOURITE FOOD: ANYTHING THAT HAS
OR HAS EVER HAD CELLULAR STRUCTURE
NAUGHTIEST DEED: PRESENTING MEL WITH A LARGE
DEAD FISH THAT SHE HAD PLUCKED FROM THE DAM
FAVOURITE PASTIME: GENERALLY BEING UNDERFOOT

MITCH

FAVOURITE TOY: TENNIS BALLS
FAVOURITE PASTIME: SLEEPING
NAUGHTIEST DEED: WHAT MALE
DOGS DO TO VISITORS' CAR TYRES
OWNERS: FRANK AND JAN MITCHELL
PET HATE: BIRDS AROUND HIS FOOD
FAVOURITE FOODS: LAMB SHANKS AND BEEF MINCE
OBSESSION: HIS DAILY RIDE IN THE UTE TO CHECK CATTLE

OWNER: AMY SMITH
FAVOURITE TOY: TEDDY
FAVOURITE FOOD: EVELYN'S BREAKFAST
PET HATES: CAR WINDOWS AND THE GARDEN HOSE
FAVOURITE PASTIMES: CHASING STICKS OUT INTO THE
RIVER AND PLAYING FETCH WITH HIS SQUEAKY TOYS
OBSESSION: MAKING LOVE TO HIS BED AFTER EVERY MEAL
NAUGHTIEST DEED: JUMPING OUT OF A CAR WINDOW AT SPEED

OWNER: ANDREW SMITH
PET HATES: DIETS AND DISCIPLINE
FAVOURITE PASTIMES: A 5-KM RUN
FOLLOWED BY A SWIM IN THE POOL
OBSESSION: GOING 'CRACKADOG' (BARKING
OBSESSIVELY WHILE RUNNING IN CIRCLES)
NAUGHTIEST DEED: PUTTING SIX NEW HOLES
IN A NEW PAIR OF JEANS IN FIVE MINUTES
FAVOURITE TOY: INDESTRUCTIBLE TOYS (WHICH HE DESTROYS)

BEAR

MARLO

FAVOURITE PASTIME: BEING AT THE BEACH
FAVOURITE FOODS: A JUICY STEAK OR BONE
FAVOURITE TOYS: FRISBEE AND A TOY KOALA
OWNERS: KRISTEN, TOM AND FRANKIE WILKS
PET HATES: THUNDER, LAWNMOWERS AND ARC WELDERS
OBSESSIONS: LICKING HIS PAWS AND BEING FIRST OUT THE DOOR
NAUGHTIEST DEEDS: SLEEPING ON THE BEDS WHEN NO ONE'S
HOME AND GREETING CUSTOMERS RATHER LOUDLY UPON ARRIVAL

BOB

FAVOURITE FOOD: BONES
OBSESSION: JASPER THE CAT
FAVOURITE TOY: TENNIS BALLS
PET HATE: BEING LEFT AT HOME
OWNERS: DARREN HAUNOLD AND SUZANNE STRAPP
FAVOURITE PASTIME: ROUNDING UP JASPER THE
CAT AND WILLS DOMAIN RESTAURANT WAITSTAFF
NAUGHTIEST DEED: STEALING VINEYARD WORKERS' LUNCHES

PET HATE: BEING LEFT AT HOME
FAVOURITE TOY: JASPER THE CAT
NAUGHTIEST DEED: RIPPING UP A
SOLAR-POWERED NODDING PANDA TOY
FAVOURITE PASTIME: DESTROYING THE BACKYARD
OBSESSION: STEALING THE CHILDREN'S SOFT TOYS
OWNERS: DARREN HAUNOLD AND SUZANNE STRAPP

POPPY

SCOOTER

OBSESSION: ROCKS
NAUGHTIEST DEED: ESCAPING
FAVOURITE PASTIME: SLEEPING
PET HATE: BIG DEANO TAKING HER BONE
FAVOURITE FOOD: LAMB AND PINOT NOIR
FAVOURITE TOYS: ROCKS AND HAZELL'S TOYS
OWNERS: SUE DIXON AND TERRY JONGEBLOED

Summer diary

Yesterday I read the newspaper.

It sucked the life out of me

A feeling of gloomy bitterness and futility dragged me to the floor.

The dog came and began to lick my face

After about five minutes of licking, hope started to return to my body;

... not much, but enough for me to be able to slowly sit up and say, "good dog"

Leunig

LEROY

OWNER: FINN KRIEL
FAVOURITE TOY: SOCKS
FAVOURITE FOOD: PEOPLE FOOD
FAVOURITE PASTIME: PINCHING SOCKS
OBSESSION: HIDING UNDER FURNITURE
NAUGHTIEST DEED: SNEAKING ONTO THE BEDS AT NIGHT
PET HATE: BEING CARRIED AROUND BY SEVEN-YEAR-OLD GIRLS

OBSESSION: PONYTAILS
OWNER: ZOE CRITTENDEN
FAVOURITE TOY: PONYTAILS
PET HATE: BEING LEFT ALONE
FAVOURITE FOOD: TOO BUSY TO EAT
FAVOURITE PASTIME: TEARING AROUND THE HOUSE
NAUGHTIEST DEED: DISTRIBUTING TOILET PAPER AROUND THE HOUSE

RUBIK

SOLLY

OWNER: VANYA CULLEN
FAVOURITE TOY: A COMFY COUCH
PET HATE: BEING INSIDE FOR TOO LONG
OBSESSION: CATCHING NOISY BLOWFLIES
FAVOURITE FOODS: LAMB CHOPS AND FISH
FAVOURITE PASTIME: CHASING SEAGULLS ON THE BEACH
NAUGHTIEST DEEDS: BREAKING HEARTS AND SITTING ON THE COUCH

PET HATE: BATHS
OBSESSION: RUBBER DUCKIES
FAVOURITE FOOD: SCHMACKOS
FAVOURITE TOY: SOCCER BALLS
NAUGHTIEST DEED: BEING CAUGHT IN A
COUPLE OF LOCAL WINERIES' FOUNTAINS
OWNERS: DANIEL, NATALIE AND JACQUES BINET
FAVOURITE PASTIME: GETTING TUMMY RUBS AT CELLAR DOOR

CHARLOTTE

RARNI

OWNER: JULIAN SCOTT
FAVOURITE TOY: STICKS
FAVOURITE FOOD: LAMB CHOPS
PET HATES: THUNDER AND THE FORKLIFT
FAVOURITE PASTIME: CHASING STICKS AND BUNGS
OBSESSION: DIGGING MASSIVE HOLES AT THE BEACH
NAUGHTIEST DEED: HIDING WHEN SHE DOESN'T WANT TO GO TO WORK

LOFTY

PET HATE: DIETS
OBSESSION: FOOD
FAVOURITE TOY: ANYTHING OF RANGER'S
NAUGHTIEST DEED: EATING RANGER'S TOYS
FAVOURITE PASTIMES: EATING AND CUDDLING
FAVOURITE FOOD: CHEF'S SOUS-VIDE CHICKEN
OWNERS: SHARON PEARSON AND GARRY SWEENEY

RANGER

PET HATE: GARBAGE TRUCK
FAVOURITE PASTIMES: PLAYING FETCH
AND SWIMMING LAPS IN THE DAM
OBSESSIONS: FETCH AND SWIMMING
FAVOURITE TOY: ANYTHING THAT SQUEAKS
NAUGHTIEST DEED: ROLLING IN KANGAROO POO
OWNERS: SHARON PEARSON AND GARRY SWEENEY
FAVOURITE FOOD: ANYTHING STOLEN OFF THE BENCH

From left:

BELLA *OWNER: RENÉE McCARTHY*
FAVOURITE PASTIME: KISSING OLIVE
NAUGHTIEST DEED: STEALING SLIPPERS
PET HATE: WALKING INTO A CROWDED ROOM

BRYNEE *OWNER: LEWIS MAXWELL*
OBSESSION: DEMANDING CUDDLES
FAVOURITE PASTIME: RUNNING THROUGH THE GARDEN
FAVOURITE TOY: FLUFFY CHICKEN

OLIVE *OWNER: MARK MAXWELL*
PET HATE: BATHS
OBSESSION: TRYING TO TALK
NAUGHTIEST DEED: TRYING TO UPSTAGE
SOPHIE AT THE PHOTO SHOOT

SOPHIE *OWNER: MARK MAXWELL*
FAVOURITE FOOD: BIKKIES
PET HATE: BEING CAUGHT ON THE BED
FAVOURITE PASTIME: SITTING IN THE BACK SEAT OF THE UTE

FAVOURITE TOY: HIS PAWS
FAVOURITE FOOD: CHICKEN
OWNERS: BRIAN FLETCHER AND DOONE MCALARY
OBSESSION: SITTING ON ANYTHING BUT THE FLOOR
NAUGHTIEST DEED: RAIDING THE BIN IN THE BATHROOM
FAVOURITE PASTIMES: SLEEPING OR TRAVELLING IN THE CAR
PET HATE: JULIUS THE CAT (HIS NEMESIS) WHO LIVES DOWN THE LANE

BART

PET HATE: WATER
OBSESSION: HIS BALL
FAVOURITE FOOD: BONES
FAVOURITE PASTIME: CHASING HIS BALL
OWNERS: AMANDA KEADY AND CAROL FALLON
NAUGHTIEST DEEDS: CHEWING A MATTRESS
AND OPENING A CARTON OF BEER

OLAF

BOON

OBSESSION: FOOD
FAVOURITE TOY: HIS BLANKET
OWNERS: GLEN AND ANNA RYAN
PET HATES: BEING LEFT OUTSIDE AND DIETING
FAVOURITE FOOD: EVERYTHING THAT'S NOT DOG FOOD
FAVOURITE PASTIMES: SNACKING AND GOING TO WORK
NAUGHTIEST DEED: NEVER POOING IN THE DESIGNATED AREA

NUDGE

FAVOURITE TOY: UGG BOOTS
OWNERS: ALEX AND RICHO BRAMSTON
NAUGHTIEST DEED: BREAKING INTO CARS
TO STEAL VINEYARD WORKERS' LUNCHES
FAVOURITE FOODS: BILTONG AND SWEET POTATO
OBSESSION: FLUSHING BIRD NETS IN THE VINEYARD
FAVOURITE PASTIME: CHASING DUCKS AROUND THE DAM

GRACIE

PET HATE: WATER
FAVOURITE PASTIME: SLEEPING
FAVOURITE TOY: TUG-OF-WAR ROPE
OWNERS: GREG AND KERRY EDMUNDS
NAUGHTIEST DEEDS: BURPING AND FARTING
OBSESSION: CHASING BIRDS IN THE GARDEN

EDIE

NAUGHTIEST DEED: FARTING
FAVOURITE PASTIME: SUNBAKING
OWNERS: CHRIS AND TEGAN TYRRELL
FAVOURITE FOOD: BROCCOLI STALKS
OBSESSION: PLAYING WITH
BABY HENRY TYRRELL AND HIS TOYS
FAVOURITE TOY: STAR WARS STORM TROOPER

CASSIE

OBSESSION: ROLLING IN MUD
PET HATE: WHIPPER SNIPPERS
FAVOURITE FOOD: FRANKFURTS
FAVOURITE TOY: ANY TYPE OF BALL
FAVOURITE PASTIME: WATCHING TV
OWNERS: GREG AND KERRY EDMUNDS
NAUGHTIEST DEED: STEALING GRACIE'S TOYS

CAESAR

OWNER: COLLEEN JREISSATI
PET HATES: LOVE AND AFFECTION
FAVOURITE PASTIME: TRAVELLING ON THE
BOW OF THE YACHT WITH THE WIND IN HIS FACE
NAUGHTIEST DEED: FIGHTING OFF A BLUE-TONGUE
LIZARD FOR THE REMNANTS OF A DEAD FROG
FAVOURITE FOOD: ANYTHING HE'S NOT MEANT TO HAVE
FAVOURITE TOY: A PINK BUNNY NAMED BUNNY WHICH HE LOVES TO 'KILL'
OBSESSION: HIS 'LOLLY BAG' WHICH HE CARRIES EVERYWHERE WITH HIM

FAVOURITE TOYS: LUXEY AND DONKEY
OBSESSION: HUNTING RABBITS AND MICE
OWNERS: PAUL BRIDGEMAN AND CAROLINE MOONEY
FAVOURITE PASTIME: SEASONALLY ADJUSTED
SLEEPING IN FRONT OF THE FIRE OR AIR CONDITIONER
FAVOURITE FOOD: ANYTHING THAT WILL RESULT IN FEELING QUEASY
PET HATE: ENFORCED DOONA-DAYS FROM GOING TOO HARD AT WORK
NAUGHTIEST DEED: EATING UNSPEAKABLE THINGS THEN LICKING FACES

ARCHIE

BANJO

PET HATE: DAYS OFF
OWNER: TOM LOVELOCK
FAVOURITE TOY: KELPIE BESTIE NAMED JARRAH
OBSESSION: CHASING BALLS, CHEWING BALLS,
DESTROYING BALLS, ASKING "WHERE'S MY BALL GONE?"
FAVOURITE PASTIME: RIDING IN THE BACK OF A UTE
FAVOURITE FOOD: ANYTHING UNFIT FOR CONSUMPTION
NAUGHTIEST DEED: SAMPLING TOO MUCH OF THE PINOT NOIR

OBSESSION: THE SOUND OF THE QUAD BIKE
OWNERS: CHAR AND TRU BURGESS-MOORE
PET HATE: BEING TOLD OFF FOR EATING GRAPES
FAVOURITE PASTIME: ROUNDING UP CUSTOMERS
AND ESCORTING THEM TO CELLAR DOOR
NAUGHTIEST DEED: DOING LAPS IN THE NEIGHBOUR'S
DAM TO SWIM WITH THE MOOREBANK GEESE
(WHO MOVED THERE TO GET AWAY FROM HER)
FAVOURITE FOOD: FRESHLY LAID EGGS FROM THE HEN HOUSE

STELLA

OSCAR

PET HATE: NONE - HE IS A LOVER, NOT A HATER
FAVOURITE TOY: CAN'T MUSTER ENERGY FOR TOYS
FAVOURITE PASTIME: LYING UPSIDE DOWN ON THE
SOFA IN CELLAR DOOR WITH HIS PAWS IN THE AIR
NAUGHTIEST DEED: STEALING FOOD OFF THE TABLE
OWNERS: LOUISE HEMSLEY-SMITH AND JOCH BOSWORTH
OBSESSION: NO SUCH THING WHEN YOU ARE THIS LAID BACK

OBSESSION: FOOD, FOOD, FOOD
NAUGHTIEST DEED: KILLING THREE
CHOOKS WHEN SHE FIRST ARRIVED
FAVOURITE PASTIMES: EATING AND
BARKING AT CELLAR DOOR CUSTOMERS
FAVOURITE FOODS: FRUIT, VEGETABLES AND CARRION
OWNERS: LOUISE HEMSLEY-SMITH AND JOCH BOSWORTH
PET HATES: BRENTON THE AUSTRALIA POST GUY AND JOCH

CONNIE

CANNUBI

PET HATE: BATHS
OBSESSION: FOOD
FAVOURITE FOOD: FRUIT
FAVOURITE PASTIME: ESCAPING
OWNERS: JO MARSH AND GLENN JAMES
NAUGHTIEST DEED: STEALING FOOD FROM OFF THE KITCHEN COUNTER

THELMA

FAVOURITE FOOD: BANANAS
PET HATE: BEING TOLD WHAT TO DO
FAVOURITE TOY: CANNUBI'S COLLAR
OWNERS: JO MARSH AND GLENN JAMES
OBSESSIONS: FOOD AND CUDDLING CANNUBI
FAVOURITE PASTIME: WALLOWING IN HER WATER BOWL
NAUGHTIEST DEED: RIPPING THE CARDBOARD ON WINE CARTONS

BiLLY BUTTON WINES BRIGHT, VIC | LABRADOR 6 & MINIATURE PIG 2 MONTHS

THINGS THAT MATTER.

What are the famous people reading this summer? What are they eating and drinking? Where are they going and what are they doing to relax? What brand of toilet paper are they using? Who cares and what does it matter?

So now to more important and useful information regarding the festive season: information about dogs; information which you could have easily overlooked or forgotten :—

THE LABRADOR IS A GREAT EATING AND DRINKING COMPANION !

The Staffordshire Bull Terrier loves to sing and is an excellent, lively and agreeable conversationalist.

The Fox Terrier is a fabulous dancer; loves a good time and is always last to leave the party. What more can be said? HAPPY NEW YEAR !

Leunig

From left:

CHILLI OWNERS: SHANE HOLLOWAY AND FRANCINE AUSTIN
OBSESSION: SLEEPING IN OBSCURE WARM PLACES
PET HATES: YOUNG DOGS AND BATHTIME
FAVOURITE PASTIME: SLEEPING
FAVOURITE TOY: CORKS

PANDA OWNER: RHYS ROBINSON
OBSESSIONS: RATTY AND ANYTHING WITH FEATHERS
NAUGHTIEST DEED: CHASING GUINEA FOWL
FAVOURITE PASTIME: CHASING BIRDS
FAVOURITE FOOD: OLD CARCASS

SCOUT OWNER: RHYS ROBINSON
FAVOURITE PASTIMES: CHASING WALLABIES
PET HATE: BEING TIED UP DUE TO WALLABY CHASING
OBSESSION: WALLABIES
FAVOURITE FOOD: CHICKEN

LULU OWNER: PAUL CHYNOWETH
OBSESSION: OPEN DOORS
NAUGHTIEST DEED: REMOVING
AND HIDING DRAIN COVERS
FAVOURITE PASTIME: SLEEPING
PET HATE: WIND

DARCY OWNERS: VAUGHN DELL AND LINDA MORICE
FAVOURITE PASTIME: HANGING OUT AT THE WINERY
NAUGHTIEST DEED: ESCAPING NEARLY EVERY DAY
FAVOURITE FOOD: FRESH CHICKEN
FAVOURITE TOY: TEDDY BEARS

MURRAY OWNERS: HANNAH HARMS AND DAN LIZOTTE
FAVOURITE PASTIME: ESCORTING CUSTOMERS
FROM THE CAR PARK TO THE CELLAR DOOR
OBSESSIONS: SWIMMING AND FOOT HYGIENE
NAUGHTIEST DEED: EATING 12 SAUSAGES
OFF THE HOT BBQ PLATE
PET HATE: HOSES

BONNIE OWNER: ALICE COOKSLEY AND ALEXANDER HALL
FAVOURITE PASTIME: CHASING BUTTERFLIES
NAUGHTIEST DEED: BARKING AT WINERY MACHINERY
OBSESSIONS: TRUCKS, BIRDS AND ANYTHING FAST
PET HATE: HAVING TO SIT STILL

BARKLEY

PET HATE: FENCES
FAVOURITE PASTIME: CUDDLING
FAVOURITE TOY: GRAPEVINE CANES
OBSESSION: CHASING KANGAROOS,
FOXES, RABBITS AND HORSES
OWNERS: MEAGAN AND JAMES BECKER
FAVOURITE FOOD: PEDIGREE DENTASTIX

OWNER: MARTY EDWARDS
PET HATE: NOT COMING TO WORK
KNOWN ACCOMPLICES: JIMMY THE CHEF
FAVOURITE TOYS: RABBITS AND PARROTS
FAVOURITE PASTIME: CHECKING THE CABERNET VINES
FAVOURITE FOOD: 40-DAY DRY AGED HEREFORD BEEF
OBSESSION: RUBBING AGAINST CLEAN BLACK CLOTHING
NAUGHTIEST DEED: INVITING HIMSELF INTO THE RESTAURANT FOR CUDDLES

ZUMA

NELLIE

FAVOURITE TOY: PEOPLE
OWNERS: DOUG AND CORRIE COX
NAUGHTIEST DEEDS: TEARING UP FOOTWEAR
AND PASSING WIND AT INOPPORTUNE MOMENTS
FAVOURITE FOOD: ANYTHING THAT THE CAT GETS
OBSESSIONS: DRONES, LARGE CAMERAS AND SKATEBOARDS
PET HATE: WHEN TIGER THE CAT COMES NEAR THE CELLAR DOOR
FAVOURITE PASTIMES: PLAYING IN THE GRAPEVINE NETS AND WRESTLING

ENTRANCE

PET HATE: WATER
OBSESSION: FOLLOWING STEVE
FAVOURITE FOOD: DEAD RABBITS
FAVOURITE TOY: WALLABY SKELETONS
OWNERS: STEVE AND MONIQUE LUBIANA
NAUGHTIEST DEED: EATING STAFF LUNCHES
FAVOURITE PASTIME: MORNING WALKS IN THE VINEYARD

JAFFA

KELPIE 7 | STEFANO LUBIANA WINES GRANTON TAS 83

OWNER: RITA TOKAR
FAVOURITE TOY: BUNGS
OBSESSION: CHASING RABBITS
NAUGHTIEST DEED: BRINGING A DEAD RABBIT TO THE CELLAR DOOR
PET HATES: WHITE UTES AND PEOPLE WHO DON'T STOP AND PAT HIM
FAVOURITE FOOD: FOOD FROM THE RESTAURANT (THE CHEFS SPOIL HIM)
FAVOURITE PASTIMES: SLEEPING IN THE SUN AND SUPERVISING IN THE VINEYARD

ALFIE

FAVOURITE TOY: TEDDY BEAR
OWNERS: BRIONY AND TONY HOARE
PET HATE: CHICKENS EATING HIS FOOD
OBSESSIONS: KANGAROOS AND CHICKENS
FAVOURITE FOODS: PIZZA OR TURKEY NECKS
NAUGHTIEST DEED: EATING HIS OWNERS' STEAKS AT DINNER
FAVOURITE PASTIMES: SLEEPING OR BARKING AT KANGAROOS

SPRITZ

ANGUS

OWNER: WENDY BULLER
PET HATE: PEOPLE SNEEZING
FAVOURITE PASTIMES: SUNBAKING
AND WELCOMING VISITORS
FAVOURITE FOOD: MARMALADE ON TOAST
OBSESSION: BEING THE ALPHA MALE AT ALL TIMES
NAUGHTIEST DEED: EATING A BAKED CHEESECAKE
WHILE IT WAS COOLING ON THE DINING ROOM TABLE

HUNTER

OWNER: ALEXANDER BULLER
FAVOURITE TOYS: WENDY'S
DRESSING GOWN AND SLIPPERS
NAUGHTIEST DEED: EATING WENDY'S
DRESSING GOWN AND SLIPPERS
OBSESSION: RIDING IN THE FRONT
SEAT WHEN HITCHING A RIDE INTO TOWN
FAVOURITE PASTIME: ANNOYING THE ROOSTER

RUEBEN

FAVOURITE FOOD: CHEESE
OWNER: ELIZABETH BULLER
FAVOURITE TOY: SQUEAKY TOY
NAUGHTIEST DEED: CHASING AND
CATCHING BABY RABBITS
FAVOURITE PASTIME: BARKING AT
POSSUMS IN THE MIDDLE OF THE NIGHT
PET HATES: LAWNMOWER AND STORMS

RICK • BURGE

BURGE FAMILY WINEMAKERS

FAVOURITE TOY: DUDLEY
OBSESSION: BEING FIRST
FAVOURITE FOOD: CHICKEN NECKS
OWNERS: RICK AND BRONNIE BURGE
PET HATE: NOT GETTING ENOUGH ATTENTION
NAUGHTIEST DEED: EATING A SPECIAL TERRINE IN THE CAR
FAVOURITE PASTIME: RIDING IN THE CAR WITH THE WINDOW DOWN

FAVOURITE FOOD: ROO MINCE
OWNERS: RICK AND BRONNIE BURGE
OBSESSION: DOING HIS SIGNATURE OTTER IMPRESSION
PET HATES: HAIRDRYERS AND NOISY TWO-YEAR-OLDS
FAVOURITE PASTIME: CUDDLING IN BED WITH BRONNIE
FAVOURITE TOY: DEREK, A BARELY RECOGNISABLE CLOTH TOY

JESS

PET HATE: FOXES
FAVOURITE TOY: BALL
OWNER: ZANE WOODBURY
FAVOURITE FOOD: RABBITS
OBSESSION: CHASING STICKS
KNOWN ACCOMPLICE: WALLY
FAVOURITE PASTIME: CHASING STICKS

HAGRID

OWNER: PIP BATTLEY
OBSESSION: CUDDLES
FAVOURITE PASTIME: ROUNDING
UP BEES INSTEAD OF SHEEP
NAUGHTIEST DEED: STEALING
FOOD OFF PEOPLE'S PLATES AT PARTIES
PET HATE: DISCIPLINE OF ANY SORT
FAVOURITE FOODS: BITS OF WOOD AND RUBBER

BILLIE

OWNER: PIP BATTLEY
OBSESSION: CATCHING FLIES
FAVOURITE PASTIME: CHASING
SEAGULLS AND RABBITS
FAVOURITE TOY: A GOOD BONE
FAVOURITE FOOD: BLUE CHEESE
NAUGHTIEST DEED: DISAPPEARING
FOR HOURS TO CHASE RABBITS
PET HATE: HER LITTLE BROTHER HAGRID

OWNER: DEREK HOOPER
FAVOURITE TOY: POULTRY
OBSESSION: BELLY SCRATCHES
FAVOURITE PASTIME: LAYING IN THE LAVENDER
PET HATE: FEELING NAKED AFTER HAVING A HAIRCUT
FAVOURITE FOOD: CELLAR DOOR LEFTOVERS, ESPECIALLY SALMON
NAUGHTIEST DEED: SOMETHING TO DO WITH HIS FAVOURITE TOY...

WALLY

LEO

OBSESSION: SHEEP WORK
FAVOURITE TOY: THE BROOM
PET HATE: ENCLOSED UTE TRAYS
FAVOURITE PASTIMES: CHEWING PEOPLE'S
FEET AND SITTING ON THE BACK OF THE UTE
OWNERS: STEPHEN, ALANA AND ZARA CHAMBERS
NAUGHTIEST DEED: CHEWING CUSHIONS AND CHILDREN'S TOYS

MAX

FAVOURITE TOY: MONTY
OBSESSION: THE QUAD BIKE
PET HATE: THE VACUUM CLEANER
FAVOURITE PASTIME: GOING TO THE BEACH
OWNERS: CRAIG AND JENNIFER BRENT-WHITE
FAVOURITE FOOD: ANYTHING FROM THE DESSERT TROLLEY
NAUGHTIEST DEED: EATING THE FRONT SEAT OF THE HILUX

PET HATE: ANDREY THE CAT
OBSESSION: RUNNING WATER
FAVOURITE FOOD: SALMON SUSHI
FAVOURITE TOY: ANYTHING THAT SQUEAKS
OWNERS: CRAIG AND JENNIFER BRENT-WHITE
FAVOURITE PASTIME: SLEEPING WITH A FULL TUMMY
NAUGHTIEST DEED: JUMPING OUT OF THE HILUX TO CHASE
A RABBIT AND RUPTURING HER CRUCIATE LIGAMENT

MONTY

MOLLY

OWNER: DAN BUCKLE
PET HATE: EARLY MORNINGS
FAVOURITE TOY: TENNIS BALLS
FAVOURITE PASTIMES: CHASING
BALLS, SWIMMING AND EATING
FAVOURITE FOOD: EVERYTHING WITH
CALORIES, ESPECIALLY BBQ CHICKEN
NAUGHTIEST DEED: ROLLING IN STINKY DEAD THINGS

PET HATE: VACUUM CLEANER
FAVOURITE TOY: DUNLOP VOLLEYS
FAVOURITE FOOD: YOGHURT DROPS
FAVOURITE PASTIME: CHASING BALLS
NAUGHTIEST DEED: SNACKING ON KANGAROO POO
OWNERS: MARY O'REILLY AND ANDREA BONANNO
OBSESSIONS: BUTTERFLIES, BIRDS AND ANYTHING THAT FLIES

CHICO

OBSESSION: ANYONE WITH A BALL
PET HATE: A WASH AND BLOW DRY
OWNERS: EMMA AND SIMON DOYLE
FAVOURITE TOYS: SOCCER BALL,
TENNIS BALL, BASKETBALL... GET THE IDEA?
FAVOURITE PASTIME: RUNNING AFTER THE GATOR
FAVOURITE FOODS: MAN FOOD! STEAK, POTATOES AND BREAD

GEORGE

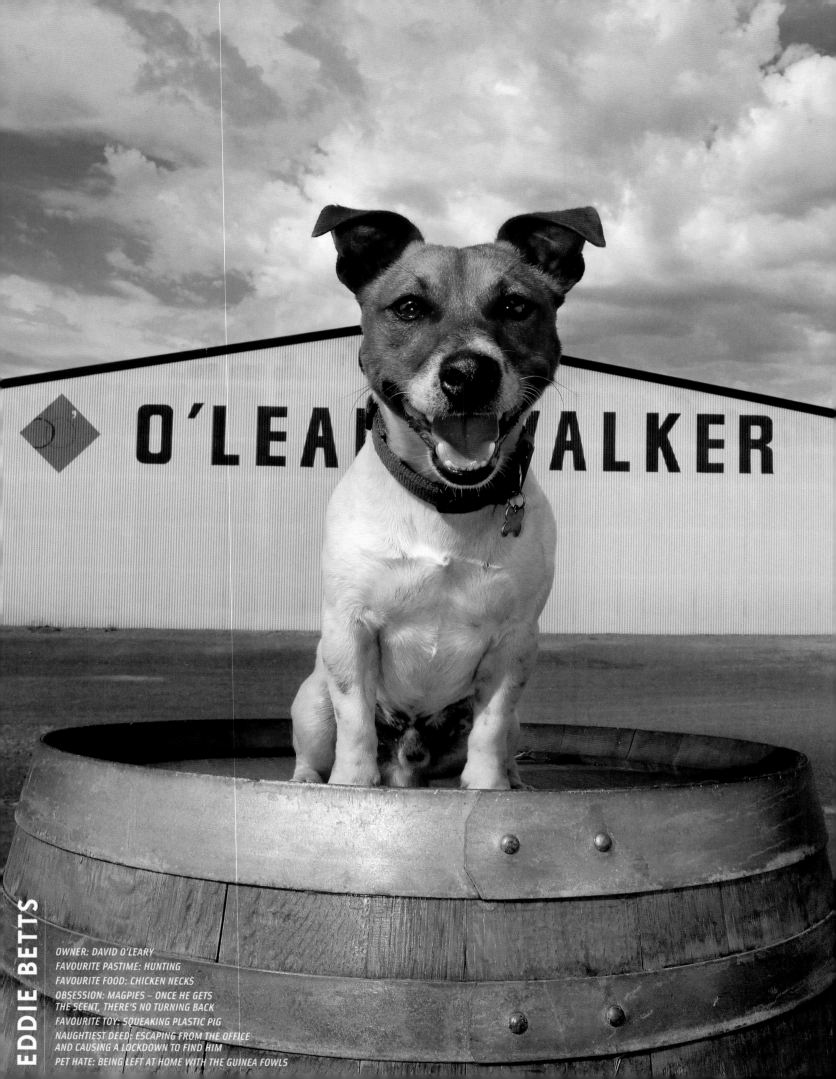

EDDIE BETTS

OWNER: DAVID O'LEARY
FAVOURITE PASTIME: HUNTING
FAVOURITE FOOD: CHICKEN NECKS
OBSESSION: MAGPIES – ONCE HE GETS
THE SCENT, THERE'S NO TURNING BACK
FAVOURITE TOY: SQUEAKING PLASTIC PIG
NAUGHTIEST DEED: ESCAPING FROM THE OFFICE
AND CAUSING A LOCKDOWN TO FIND HIM
PET HATE: BEING LEFT AT HOME WITH THE GUINEA FOWLS

the art of dogs receives very little
attention or acclaim, except, of course
from other dogs

" I liked the
statement that Rex
made on the
lamp post "

" yes but I
think his
installation on
the footpath was
bolder and more
memorable "

Leunig

NELSON

PET HATE: WATER
OWNER: MATT POOLEY
FAVOURITE TOY: KNOTTED ROPE
FAVOURITE FOOD: CHICKEN NECKS
FAVOURITE PASTIME: CHASING BIRDS
NAUGHTIEST DEED: CHEWING BLINDS
OBSESSION: CHEWING UP CLOTHES PEGS

OWNERS: PETER AND DAVE LANE
FAVOURITE FOOD: CHICKEN NECKS
FAVOURITE TOY: TUG-OF-WAR ROPE
PET HATE: HAVING HIS TAIL TOUCHED
NAUGHTIEST DEED: CHEWING THE DASH,
MUD FLAPS AND DOOR LINING OF THE UTE
OBSESSION: CHASING BIRDS UNTIL HE IS TOTALLY EXHAUSTED
FAVOURITE PASTIME: CHASING BIRDS AND RABBITS WITH NELSON

TANK

WINSTON

FAVOURITE TOY: COOPER
PET HATE: BEING COOPED UP
FAVOURITE FOOD: JUICY BONES
OBSESSION: ROUNDING UP COOPER
FAVOURITE PASTIME: EXPLORING HIS
NEW-FOUND FREEDOM AT WHISTLER
OWNERS: MARTIN AND SALLY PFEIFFER
NAUGHTIEST DEED: POKING HIS TONGUE OUT

COOPER

OWNER: JOSH PFEIFFER
FAVOURITE FOOD: ICE CREAM
FAVOURITE TOY: SOCCER BALL
PET HATES: FIREWORKS AND STORMS
NAUGHTIEST DEED: STEALING CHEESE
FROM CUSTOMERS' PLATTERS
OBSESSION: CHASING THE MOTORBIKE
FAVOURITE PASTIME: PLAYING WITH KIDS AT CELLAR DOOR

OWNER: SAM ATHERTON
PET HATE: CRYING BABIES
FAVOURITE PASTIME: SNEAKING UNDER
PEOPLE'S FEET, ESPECIALLY IN THE KITCHEN
NAUGHTIEST DEED: TEARING UP CUSHIONS
OBSESSIONS: FOOD AND GETTING UNDER PEOPLE'S FEET

SHAZZA

TICKY

OWNERS: JEN AND DAVE WRIGHT
FAVOURITE FOOD: CHICKEN FILLET
PET HATE: JEN AND DAVE SLEEPING IN
OBSESSIONS: BIRDS AND HER SQUEAKY DUCK
FAVOURITE PASTIME: SWIMMING OUT TO SEA AS FAR
AS SHE CAN GO (SHE NOW HAS HER OWN LIFE JACKET)
FAVOURITE TOYS: SQUEAKY DUCK AND UNWASHED SOCKS
NAUGHTIEST DEED: EATING MILLIPEDES THEN THROWING THEM BACK UP

OBSESSION: TINA
OWNER: TINA KIES
FAVOURITE FOOD: TURKEY NECKS
FAVOURITE PASTIMES: RIDING IN THE
CAR AND BEING AN ESCAPE ARTIST
NAUGHTIEST DEED: SETTING TRAPS
AND POUNCING WHEN HIS VICTIM ARRIVES
PET HATE: HIS SIBLINGS TAKING HIS TREATS

DIEGO

MABEL

PET HATES: LAWNMOWERS AND HOSES
OBSESSION: GUARDING HER FOOD BOWL
OWNERS: LYNNE AND MICHAEL DAL ZOTTO
FAVOURITE TOYS: THE CATS AND WEBSTER
FAVOURITE FOOD: ANYTHING AND EVERYTHING, IN ABUNDANCE
FAVOURITE PASTIME: HARASSING FELLOW DOG WEBSTER AND THE CATS
NAUGHTIEST DEED: JUMPING ON PEOPLE'S BACKS WHEN THEY LEAST EXPECT IT

OBSESSION: THE GARDEN HOSE
FAVOURITE PASTIME: CHASING BOCCE BALLS
OWNERS: CHRISTIAN AND SIMONE DAL ZOTTO
FAVOURITE TOYS: TEDDY AND MONSTER-MOUTH
FAVOURITE FOODS: PASTA, SALAMI AND PROSCIUTTO
PET HATES: THE VACCUUM CLEANER AND SAUVIGNON BLANC
NAUGHTIEST DEED: FARTING UNDER THE TABLE AT DINNER PARTIES

ARNOLD

SUNNY

OWNER: BEN DE BORTOLI
FAVOURITE FOOD: DORITOS
PET HATE: BEING WASHED
FAVOURITE PASTIME: ROAD TRIPS
FAVOURITE TOY: TUG-O-WAR ROPE
OBSESSION: CHASING KANGAROOS
NAUGHTIEST DEED: HIJACKING VISITORS' CARS

PET HATE: VISITING THE VET
OWNERS: STEPHEN AND LEANNE WEBBER
OBSESSION: LYING RIGHT IN FRONT OF THE
DOOR SO EVERYONE HAS TO STEP OVER HER
FAVOURITE FOOD: LEFTOVER SCOTCH FILLET FROM THE BBQ
FAVOURITE PASTIMES: EATING AND SLEEPING AND EATING...

MISSY

HAMISH

OWNER: NAT BURCH
FAVOURITE PASTIME: SLEEPING
FAVOURITE FOOD: REDISCOVERED BONES
FAVOURITE TOY: KONG WITH PEANUT BUTTER
PET HATES: GRASS SEEDS AND BEING PICKED UP
NAUGHTIEST DEED: PLAYING MIND GAMES WITH VEHICLES
OBSESSIONS: FLIES AND PROTECTING THE HOUSE AT NIGHT

LORENZO

OBSESSION: WATER
OWNER: SAM MIRANDA
PET HATE: BIRD SCARERS
FAVOURITE PASTIME: WATER
FAVOURITE TOY: WATER HOSE
NAUGHTIEST DEED: BITING THE PRESSURE WASHER NOZZLE

SAAZ

OBSESSION: BRIONI
OWNER: CORRINA WRIGHT
FAVOURITE TOY: PATTERSON'S BUNG
PET HATE: BEING WOKEN UP AT HOME TIME
FAVOURITE PASTIMES: SLEEPING AND SNORING
FAVOURITE FOOD: DRIPPINGS ON THE GROUND
AFTER A PORCHETTA PARTY PIG ON THE SPIT
NAUGHTIEST DEED: ROLLING IN DEAD THINGS
AND SLOBBERING ON PEOPLE'S GOING-OUT CLOTHES

PATTERSON

OBSESSION: BRIONI
OWNER: BRIONI OLIVER
FAVOURITE TOY: BUNGS
FAVOURITE PASTIME: BARKING AT
ANYONE WHO GOES NEAR THE UTE
FAVOURITE FOOD: PORCHETTA PARTY LEFTOVERS
NAUGHTIEST DEED: RUNNING AWAY TO LOOK FOR BRIONI
PET HATE: BEING LEFT AT CELLAR DOOR WITHOUT BRIONI

CURLY

NAUGHTIEST DEED: STEALING
AND THEN DESTROYING THONGS
AND INNER SOLES FROM SHOES
OBSESSIONS: RUNNING AND BOUNCING
PET HATES: THUNDER AND BEING ALONE
FAVOURITE PASTIMES: CHASING
RABBITS AND ESCAPING FROM HIS YARD
OWNERS: WAYNE AND MICHELLE STEHBENS
FAVOURITE FOODS: CHICKEN AND CARROTS

OWNERS: ANDREW AND HOLLY MARSH
FAVOURITE TOY: POPPY MARSH, WHOSE
CURLY HAIR REMINDS HIM OF A SHEEP
OBSESSION: CHASING BEAR ON HIS SCOOTER
PET HATES: BROOMS AND VACUUM CLEANERS
FAVOURITE PASTIME: CHASING HIS BEST FRIEND
BEN UP THE GOLF COURSE EVERY AFTERNOON
FAVOURITE FOOD: STINKY DEAD KANGAROO LEGS
NAUGHTIEST DEED: WAKING UP THE NEIGHBOURS
AT 6AM BY BARKING AT HOT AIR BALLOONS

SPOOK

From left:

ZEPHYR *OWNER: PHIL HUTCHISON*
FAVOURITE FOOD: PIG'S EARS
OBSESSION: HANGING OUT WITH HIS OWNER
PET HATES: PLASTIC BAGS AND LEAF BLOWERS
FAVOURITE PASTIMES: SLEEPING AND SUNBATHING
NAUGHTIEST DEED: DESTROYING
A FEATHER-CUSHIONED COUCH

PINOT *OWNER: TIM LOVETT*
OBSESSION: EMUS
FAVOURITE PASTIMES: RUNNING IN THE
VINEYARD AND PEEING ON CAR TYRES
FAVOURITE FOODS: CHICKEN AND RICE
NAUGHTIEST DEED: FOUR BREAK & ENTERS
PET HATES: THUNDER AND GINGER CATS

AGGIE *OWNERS: GREG, SAM AND EDIE BYERS*
FAVOURITE PASTIME: SLEEPING ON THE COUCH
OBSESSION: SEAGULLS
PET HATE: SKATEBOARDERS
FAVOURITE FOOD: LEFTOVERS
FAVOURITE TOY: EDIE'S TOY RABBIT
NAUGHTIEST DEED: RIPPING UP A 10KG
BAG OF FLOUR IN THE LIVING ROOM

TOBY

OWNER: MICHAEL SAWYER
FAVOURITE FOODS: CHEESE, BANANAS AND STEAK
PET HATES: THUNDER, BEING BRUSHED AND POSSUMS
FAVOURITE TOY: AN EMPTY POT THAT HE CAN PUSH AROUND
FAVOURITE PASTIMES: GOING FOR WALKS AND MEETING PEOPLE
OBSESSION: BARKING AT POSSUMS, BIRDS AND HOT AIR BALLOONS
NAUGHTIEST DEED: STEALING UNDERWEAR FROM VISITORS' SUITCASES

SALLY

OWNER: ALEX FINNIE
PET HATE: GETTING IN THE CAR
FAVOURITE TOY: STICKS — THE BIGGER, THE BETTER
OBSESSION: BARKING AT DRAGONFLIES DOWN AT THE DAM
FAVOURITE FOOD: ANYTHING DROPPED AT LUNCH EXCEPT LETTUCE
FAVOURITE PASTIME: GUIDING WALKERS ON THE WINERY RIDGE WALK
NAUGHTIEST DEED: SLEEPING ON THE COUCH AFTER EVERYONE HAS GONE TO BED

OWNER: ANTON GROFFEN
FAVOURITE FOOD: OVERGROWN CUCUMBERS
OBSESSION: CHASING KANGAROOS OR FLIES
FAVOURITE TOYS: LEGO OR ANYTHING MADE OF RUBBER
NAUGHTIEST DEEDS: HARVESTING VEGETABLES AND
SNEAKING BEHIND THE FORKLIFT WITHOUT WEARING HI-VIZ
PET HATE: HAVING TO JUMP BACK ON THE UTE AFTER A BIG DAY
FAVOURITE PASTIME: LYING ON THE TRAMPOLINE WHILE CHEWING CUCUMBERS

BARNEY

OLLIE

PET HATE: BATHTIME
FAVOURITE TOY: COLIN THE CAT
OWNERS: THE TROTTER FAMILY
FAVOURITE FOOD: ROAST CHICKEN
OBSESSIONS: PEOPLE, OTHER DOGS AND COLIN THE CAT
FAVOURITE PASTIMES: RUNNING AND EXPLORING THROUGH THE VINES
NAUGHTIEST DEED: EATING THE PET FISH AFTER HE BROKE THE FISH BOWL

OBSESSION: EXERCISE
OWNER: HAYDEN TINKLER
PET HATE: BEING LEFT AT HOME
FAVOURITE TOY: STUFFED BUNNY
FAVOURITE FOOD: MUSCAT GRAPES
NAUGHTIEST DEED: BARKING NONSTOP IN THE UTE
FAVOURITE PASTIME: KEEPING IAN TINKLER COMPANY IN THE UTE

BANE

MAEVE

OBSESSION: LICKING FAY THE WINE CAT
FAVOURITE FOODS: SEAFOOD AND APPLES
OWNERS: LYNDA, PAUL AND ISAAC WILLIAMS
FAVOURITE PASTIME: CARRYING STICKS OR TEDDIES
PET HATE: BEING RESTRAINED FROM GREETING GUESTS
NAUGHTIEST DEED: EATING TWO RAW PIZZA DOUGH BASES
FAVOURITE TOYS: CHRISTMAS TEDDY, PIG AND WOBBLY BIRD

OWNER: JEZ HODGSON
FAVOURITE TOY: A FRISBEE THAT FLOATS
NAUGHTIEST DEED: STEALING AN
ENTIRE WHEEL OF CHEESE OFF THE TABLE
PET HATES: BAGS OF ICE AND FROZEN PEAS
FAVOURITE FOODS: CHICKEN NECKS AND CHEESE
OBSESSIONS: STICKS, BALLS, BUNGS AND FRISBEES
FAVOURITE PASTIMES: DOING BOMBIES OFF THE JETTY
AND ROUNDING UP THE PLASTIC COWS IN COWARAMUP

BILLIE

ZIGGY

FAVOURITE FOOD: CHEESE
OWNER: LUKE ECKERSLEY
OBSESSION: FOLLOWING LUKE
PET HATES: CATS AND CHICKENS
FAVOURITE TOY: IKE THE TOY DOGGY
FAVOURITE PASTIME: SLEEPING ON THE COUCH
NAUGHTIEST DEED: CATCHING AND EATING LOW-FLYING BIRDS

OWNER: LUKE ECKERSLEY
FAVOURITE FOOD: ITALIAN SAUSAGE
PET HATES: BALLOONS AND THUNDER
OBSESSION: GROOMING HIS SISTER ZIGGY
FAVOURITE PASTIME: SLEEPING ON THE COUCH
NAUGHTIEST DEED: DRAGGING HIS BUM ON PERSIAN RUGS

OSCAR

OBSESSION: THE BROOM
FAVOURITE TOY: THE BROOM
FAVOURITE FOOD: EGGS ON SATURDAY
PET HATE: THE SPRAY BOTTLE OF DOOM
FAVOURITE PASTIME: CHASING THE BROOM
OWNERS: BRYAN, STACY AND JORYN WIDSTRAND
NAUGHTIEST DEED: A MOUNTAIN OF EATEN SHOES

KAIRON

LEO

FAVOURITE TOY: STUFFED TEDDY BEAR
OWNERS: GRAHAM AND NADEAR WARD
NAUGHTIEST DEED: EATING THE CAT'S FOOD
OBSESSION: PLAYING WITH HIS TEDDY BEAR
PET HATES: THE CAT, LOUD NOISES AND BALLOONS
FAVOURITE PASTIMES: EATING AND GOING TO THE BEACH

IN VINO VERITAS (in wine the truth)

Ah yes; in wine there is truth; but for heaven's sake, who needs THAT?! Who wants the truth?

And at last, now it's safe for real men to drink wine and remain utterly devious.

Good news!
The science of modern oenology has developed exciting new filtering methods to remove the truth from wine after fermentation.

All good news for politics, commerce, the media and the art world—
ALL WINNERS THANKS TO MODERN SCIENCE.

Say goodbye to those terrible dinners when somebody suddenly blurted out their thoughts and ruined the evening.

The filtered-out rogue truth element becomes a by-product and is used as duck food. Ducks have no trouble digesting truth. In fact...

... they love it!

Leunig

POLLY

OBSESSION: BEING PATTED
OWNERS: DARREN AND JACKIE BROWN
NAUGHTIEST DEED: PASSING WIND IN THE CELLAR
DOOR AFTER EATING ROTTEN GUINEA FOWL EGGS
FAVOURITE FOOD: ANYTHING BUT PEAS, CARROTS AND CORN
FAVOURITE PASTIME: LAYING ON HER BACK AND BEING PATTED
PET HATE: PEOPLE USING THEIR FOOT TO PAT HER INSTEAD OF THEIR HAND

ANGUS

OWNERS: NICK AND MEL PASTODA
PET HATE: RIDING IN THE BACK OF THE UTE
FAVOURITE TOY: HIS MANGLED TEDDY BEAR
FAVOURITE PASTIME: GETTING PATS AT CELLAR DOOR
NAUGHTIEST DEED: BURYING BONES IN THE HERB GARDEN
OBSESSION: BRINGING 'PRESENTS' (RANDOM OBJECTS) TO PEOPLE

NASH

PET HATE: HAIR DRYERS
OWNER: BELLA PANNELL
FAVOURITE TOY: TENNIS BALLS
FAVOURITE PASTIME: SNUGGLING
FAVOURITE FOOD: CHINESE ROASTED DUCK
OBSESSIONS: FOLLOWING BELLA AND BEING PICKED UP LIKE A BABY
NAUGHTIEST DEED: STEALING THE KIDS' LUNCHES OUT OF THEIR BAGS

OBSESSION: POSSUMS
OWNER: FINN PANNELL
FAVOURITE PASTIME: ESCAPING
PET HATE: SLEEPING ON THE FLOOR
FAVOURITE TOY: SQUEAKY WINE BOTTLE
NAUGHTIEST DEED: EATING GLUE STICKS
FAVOURITE FOODS: AVOCADOS AND TOMATOES

BUDDHA

PORTIA

PET HATE: BEING ON A LEAD
OWNERS: THE LUSBY FAMILY
FAVOURITE FOOD: LEFTOVERS
OBSESSION: HER PINK BED MAT
FAVOURITE PASTIME: CHASING KANGAROOS
NAUGHTIEST DEED: RUNNING THROUGH A WEDDING
FAVOURITE TOY: ANY STUFFED TOY (HAS BEEN KNOWN
TO TAKE THEM FROM NEIGHBOURING PROPERTIES)

OWNER: SIMON KILLEEN
PET HATE: ANGRY VOICES
FAVOURITE FOOD: CHICKEN NECKS
FAVOURITE TOY: SQUEAKY PIG (NOW BROKEN)
OBSESSION: DRAGGING DOGS BY THEIR COLLARS
NAUGHTIEST DEED: CHEWING THE IPHONE CORD TO BITS
FAVOURITE PASTIME: FOLLOWING TILLY AROUND AND DOING AS SHE DOES

OWNER: SIMON KILLEEN
PET HATE: SQUEAKY TOYS
FAVOURITE TOY: LEFTOVER BONES
OBSESSIONS: HUNTING AND CHASING RABBITS
NAUGHTIEST DEED: EATING A TRAY OF RAT BAIT
FAVOURITE PASTIME: GOING FOR RUNS WITH SIMON
KNOWN ACCOMPLICES: JOCK, OLIVE, THE CHUG
AND HAMISH AND OSCAR THE GREY MOGGIES)

JOCK

TILLY

CHARLIE BROWN

PET HATE: ANGRY PEOPLE

FAVOURITE FOODS: ROAST CHICKEN
AND MEDIUM RARE FILLET STEAK

OWNERS: WARREN AND NICKY RANDALL

FAVOURITE PASTIME: BEING PHOTOGRAPHED
WITH CELLAR DOOR CUSTOMERS

NAUGHTIEST DEED: HUNTING NATIVE FEASTS

OBSESSIONS: POINTING AND CHASING RABBITS AT SEPPELTSFIELD

LUCY

NAUGHTIEST DEED: CHEWING THE
CORNERS OFF A SHEEPSKIN RUG

FAVOURITE TOY: LITTLE BLUE MONKEY

OWNERS: WARREN AND NICKY RANDALL

PET HATE: THE EXHAUST NOTE OF THE FERRARI

FAVOURITE FOODS: SALMON SASHIMI AND PISTACHIOS

OBSESSION: HUNTING RATS AROUND THE CHICKEN COOP

OBSESSION: BALLS
FAVOURITE TOY: HUMANS
OWNERS: FI AND COL SHEPPARD
FAVOURITE FOOD: PISTACHIO NUTS
NAUGHTIEST DEED: PEEING ON A CUSTOMER
PET HATE: FLIES (WILL LEAVE THE ROOM IF HE HEARS ONE)
FAVOURITE PASTIME: GETTING CAUGHT IN THE BIRD NETTING

GUS

OBSESSION: SOCKS
PET HATE: WILD CATS
FAVOURITE TOY: SOCKS
FAVOURITE FOOD: CHICKEN NECKS
FAVOURITE PASTIMES: LONG BEACH WALKS
AND SPEAKING FRENCH (SHE IS BILINGUAL)
OWNERS: ALAIN ROUSSEAU AND MARIE-PAULE LEROUX
NAUGHTIEST DEED: PINCHING OTHER DOGS' FOOD WHEN THEY COME AROUND TO PLAY

MALO

PET HATE: WATER PISTOLS
OWNERS: GREG AND NATALA FLYNN
FAVOURITE FOODS: STINKY OLD
MEAT OR WHATEVER PUSS IS EATING
OBSESSION: CHASING KANGAROOS
FAVOURITE TOY: KIDS' BEANIE BOOS
NAUGHTIEST DEED: GOING INTO THE KIDS'
ROOMS AND RIPPING UP THEIR TOYS
FAVOURITE PASTIME: SNEAKING ONTO THE COUCH FOR A SNOOZE

PET HATE: DIETS
FAVOURITE PASTIME: BEING BRUSHED
AND SCRATCHED ON THE BELLY
OBSESSIONS: CHILDREN AND EATING
FAVOURITE TOY: PLASTIC CONTAINER
OWNERS: GREG AND NATALA FLYNN
NAUGHTIEST DEED:
FLIRTING WITH THE STALLIONS
FAVOURITE FOOD: CARROTS

MISSY MOO

BEATRICE

PET HATE: VACUUM CLEANER
OBSESSION: CHASING SKINKS
OWNERS: SAM AND MILLIE BARRY
FAVOURITE PASTIME: SUNBAKING
FAVOURITE FOOD: POACHED EGGS
NAUGHTIEST DEED: STAYING UP PAST HER BEDTIME

MARGAUX

FAVOURITE TOY: HER PINK BUNNY
OWNERS: TOM AND OLIVIA BARRY
NAUGHTIEST DEED: MARKING HER
TERRITORY EVERYWHERE SHE GOES
PET HATE: WALKING ON WET GRASS
FAVOURITE PASTIME: LYING IN THE SUN
FAVOURITE FOOD: ANYTHING DROPPED
FROM HER HUMAN SISTER'S HIGHCHAIR

FAVOURITE TOY: BUNGS
OWNERS: DUNCAN AND JESS LOWE
FAVOURITE FOODS: CHEESE, ALMOND
CROISSANTS AND SMOKED PIG'S EARS
PET HATES: FLIES, RABBITS, SNAKES AND FOXES
FAVOURITE PASTIME: SITTING IN HIS COMFY CHAIR
ON THE VERANDA OVERSEEING VINEYARD STAFF
OBSESSION: BARKING AT WALLACE, THE VINEYARD WALLABY
NAUGHTIEST DEEDS: EATING A WHOLE CACTUS AND GIVING
SLOPPY KISSES AFTER DRINKING THE LIQUID FISH FERTILISER

LEO

JESSIE

FAVOURITE PASTIMES: PLAYING
BALL AND GREETING CUSTOMERS
OWNERS: REBECCA AND RALPH FOWLER
FAVOURITE FOOD: FROZEN CHICKEN NECKS
OBSESSION: CHASING BALLS WITH THE KIDS
KNOWN ACCOMPLICE: CHARDONNAY THE CAT
NAUGHTIEST DEED: THROWING
HER BALL IN A WINE VAT

FAVORITE WORN AND SHABBY DOMESTIC ITEMS

THE ARMCHAIR OF PHILOSOPHY.
THE TEAPOT OF TRUTH.
THE PILLOW OF FAITH.
THE RUG OF CONSTANCY.
THE VASE OF TRANQUILITY
THE DOG OF SANITY

ZOE

FAVOURITE TOY: FLUFFY RABBIT
OWNERS: JUSTIN, JULIE AND JACLIN ARDILL
FAVOURITE PASTIME: BARKING AT THE WIND
OBSESSIONS: BEING PATTED AND WONDERING
WHERE HER NEXT MEAL IS COMING FROM
PET HATES: CATS AND MISSING OUT ON FUN
NAUGHTIEST DEED: CHASING THE NEIGHBOUR'S
SHEEP UNTIL IT TURNED AROUND AND STARED HER DOWN
FAVOURITE FOOD: ANYTHING THAT MAY OR MAY NOT RESEMBLE FOOD

CHARLIE

FAVOURITE TOY: SQUEAKY PLASTIC BONE
OBSESSION: THE TWO DOGS NEXT DOOR
OWNERS: JUSTIN, JULIE AND JACLIN ARDILL
PET HATE: VISITORS DISTURBING HIS SNOOZING
NAUGHTIEST DEED: TRYING TO STOP THE GRAPE TRUCKS
BY RUNNING IN FRONT OF THEM (EVERY VINTAGE)
FAVOURITE PASTIME: SNOOZING IN THE SUN ON THE WINERY VERGE
FAVOURITE FOODS: CHEESE AND CHICKEN – PREFERABLY AT THE SAME TIME

OBSESSION: BIRDS
PET HATE: LAWNMOWERS
OWNERS: GUS AND EDDIE
FAVOURITE TOY: MINIATURE FOOTY
KNOWN ACCOMPLICE: REDDY THE CHOOK
NAUGHTIEST DEED: STEALING AND EATING BUTTER
FAVOURITE PASTIME: CHASING BIRDS IN THE VINEYARD

MOSS

JULIETTE

PET HATE: LOUD NOISES
OWNERS: WENDY AND NATASHA KILLEEN
FAVOURITE TOYS: BALLS, SQUEAKY TOYS AND STICKS
OBSESSION: LOOKING LIKE A DOG BUT THINKING LIKE A HUMAN
FAVOURITE FOOD: WINEMAKER ANDREW'S BEEF FILLET OFFCUTS
FAVOURITE PASTIME: SMOOCHING WITH CELLAR DOOR CUSTOMERS

TANNIN

PET HATE: HAVING A SHOWER
FAVOURITE TOY: PING PONG BALLS
OBSESSION: UMPIRING PING PONG
NAUGHTIEST DEED: BARKING
WHEN PEOPLE DON'T THROW TOYS
FAVOURITE PASTIME: CHASING RABBITS
FAVOURITE FOOD: FRESHLY CAUGHT RABBIT
OWNERS: BOBBIE MAKIN AND JENNIFER LAWRENCE

FAVOURITE FOOD: CHICKEN
PET HATE: WHEN CAR RIDES END
FAVOURITE TOY: TUG-O-WAR ROPE
OBSESSION: GETTING BUTT SCRATCHES
NAUGHTIEST DEED: JUMPING ON THE BENCH
TO EAT 24 FRESHLY COOKED SAUSAGES
FAVOURITE PASTIME: SWIMMING IN THE DAM
OWNERS: BOBBIE MAKIN AND JENNIFER LAWRENCE

MOLLIE

ARCHIE

PET HATE: FANCY DRESS

FAVOURITE TOY: PINE CONES

OWNERS: THE SEXTON FAMILY

FAVOURITE PASTIME: SWIMMING IN THE FROG
BOG WITH LABRADORS TILDA AND FRANKIE

OBSESSION: GREETING VISITORS WITH WARM,
WET AND GENTLE 'HANDSHAKES' (WITH HIS MOUTH)

NAUGHTIEST DEED: CRASHING THE STAGE AT
A CLASSICAL MUSIC CONCERT IN THE WINERY

FAVOURITE FOOD: RED HILL CHEESE FROM GUESTS' CHEESEBOARDS

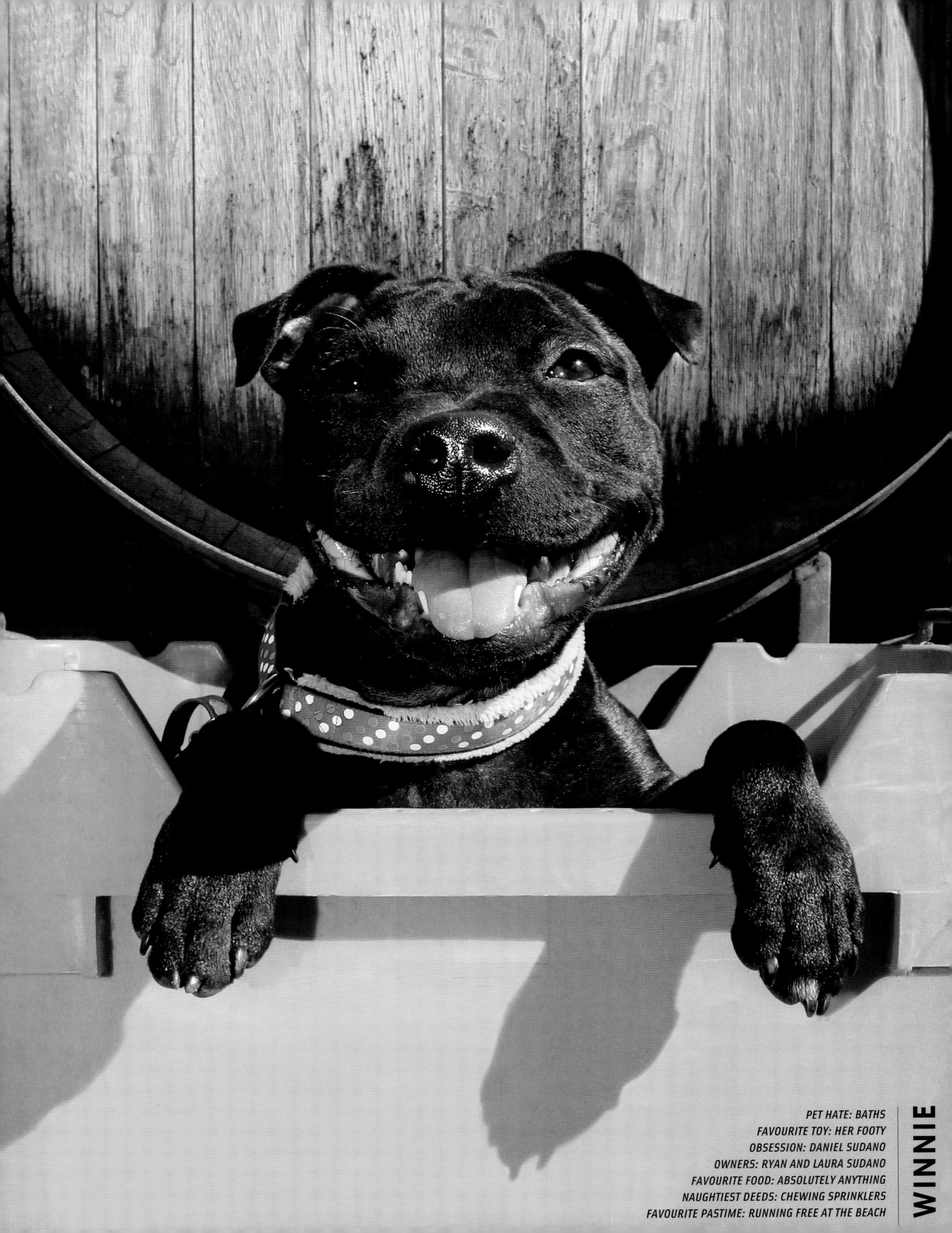

WINNIE

PET HATE: BATHS
FAVOURITE TOY: HER FOOTY
OBSESSION: DANIEL SUDANO
OWNERS: RYAN AND LAURA SUDANO
FAVOURITE FOOD: ABSOLUTELY ANYTHING
NAUGHTIEST DEEDS: CHEWING SPRINKLERS
FAVOURITE PASTIME: RUNNING FREE AT THE BEACH

PIXIE

FAVOURITE TOY: UNDERPANTS
OBSESSION: GOING TO CELLAR DOOR
OWNERS: OLA TYLESTAM AND STEPHEN JUNK
FAVOURITE PASTIME: LYING ON THE SOFA IN
THE CELLAR DOOR, WAITING FOR CUSTOMERS
NAUGHTIEST DEED: STEALING FRUIT FROM
THE ORCHARD AND RAIDING LADIES' HANDBAGS

XENA

PET HATE: SHARING A BED
WITH THE OTHER DOGS
FAVOURITE PASTIME: CHASING
BIRDS AND TENNIS BALLS
NAUGHTIEST DEED: KILLING BIRDS
OBSESSION: CHASING THE SPRINKLERS
OWNERS: OLA TYLESTAM AND STEPHEN JUNK

HUGO

PET HATE: WINE
OBSESSION: FOOD
FAVOURITE TOY: PLASTIC BOTTLES
FAVOURITE PASTIMES: CHASING ROOS AND SITTING
IN THE BACK SEAT OF THE CAR
OWNERS: OLA TYLESTAM AND STEPHEN JUNK
NAUGHTIEST DEED: EATING NESPRESSO PODS

PET HATE: CATS
FAVOURITE TOY: HIS BLANKET
OWNERS: THE BROWN FAMILY
FAVOURITE FOOD: SMOKED TROUT DIP
FAVOURITE PASTIMES: FISHING ON THE BOAT AND
PLAYING CATCH (BUT NEVER RETURNING THE BALL)
NAUGHTIEST DEED: WHAT HE DOES WITH HIS BLANKET
OBSESSION: WATCHING THE END OF THE FISHING LINE FOR
HOURS AND LICKING EACH FISH THAT ARRIVES ON THE BOAT

GUS

FAVOURITE TOY: BLOW FLIES
OWNERS: FIONA WELLER AND JULIAN ALLPORT
PET HATES: THE LAWNMOWER AND VACUUM CLEANER
NAUGHTIEST DEED: EATING PINOT NOIR GRAPES OFF THE VINE
OBSESSIONS: SUMMER: SITTING IN THE SUN, WINTER: SITTING BY THE FIRE
FAVOURITE FOOD: "IF IT'S GOOD ENOUGH FOR HUMANS, IT'S GOOD ENOUGH FOR ME"
FAVOURITE PASTIMES: CHASING SUNSHINE AND WAITING FOR CUDDLES AT CELLAR DOOR

OTTO

OWNER: GWYN OLSEN
FAVOURITE PASTIME: VISITING THE
MARKETING DEPARTMENT FOR TREATS
NAUGHTIEST DEED: STEALING A LIVE
CHICKEN FROM THE RESTAURANT NEXT
DOOR AND DELIVERING IT TO THE WINERY
FAVOURITE FOOD: PEANUT BUTTER ON TOAST
PET HATES: BRIDESMAIDS AND THE HORSES
WHO PULL THE CARTS FOR THE WINERY TOURS
ALTER EGO: BRIAR RIDGE VINEYARD WINE DOG

SPENCER

SPARKY

OBSESSION: TALKING
OWNER: AARON GOULD
FAVOURITE TOY: HYDRA
PET HATES: CIGARETTE SMOKE AND CATS
FAVOURITE FOOD: PÂTÉ ON WATER CRACKERS

OWNER: JESS ROBERTSON
FAVOURITE FOOD: CHICKEN
OBSESSION: THE SPRINKLER
PET HATE: BEING ON THE LEAD
FAVOURITE TOY: SQUEAKY DOG BONE
FAVOURITE PASTIME: CHEWING, CHEWING, CHEWING
NAUGHTIEST DEED: DESTROYING THE LOUNGE CHAIRS

HYDRA

MERLO

PET HATE: HERMES
OWNER: THE DOLAN FAMILY
FAVOURITE PASTIMES: EMPTYING THE OFFICE PAPER BINS AND JUMPING IN THE FOUNTAIN
FAVOURITE FOOD: ANYTHING THAT LOOKS LIKE FOOD
OBSESSION: BALLS, HUGS AND PLAYING WITH BILLIE
NAUGHTIEST DEEDS: VISITING WEDDING PARTIES AFTER SWIMMING IN THE POND AND EATING THE TV REMOTE

BILLIE

OWNER: TIM HOLMES
OBSESSION: SHADOWING TIM
FAVOURITE PASTIME: JOINING IN THE WINERY CRICKET AND FOOTY MATCHES
FAVOURITE FOOD: FRIDAY NIGHT TIN OF SARDINES
PET HATES: HOT AIR BALLOONS AND SQUEAKY TOYS
NAUGHTIEST DEED: SWIMMING IN THE GOLDFISH POND

HERMES

OBSESSION: THE COWS
OWNER: PETA CARLSON
FAVOURITE TOY: HIS KONG FRISBEE
PET HATE: THE HIGH-PRESSURE CLEANER
FAVOURITE FOOD: A SNEAKY BIT OF CHEESE
FAVOURITE PASTIME: BARKING AT THE COWS
NAUGHTIEST DEED: ROLLING IN KANGAROO POO

MAISIE

OWNERS: PETER AND ROZ SEPPELT
PET HATE: MISSING OUT ON ATTENTION
FAVOURITE PASTIME: BEING WHERE THE ACTION IS
OBSESSION: SITTING ON PEOPLE'S FEET FOR ATTENTION
NAUGHTIEST DEED: STEALING ROZ'S GARDENING GLOVES

MALT

FAVOURITE TOY: ANY LEAF
FAVOURITE PASTIME: SLEEPING
FAVOURITE FOOD: PETER'S PIZZA
OBSESSION: MOOCHING FOR PIZZA
OWNERS: PETER AND ROZ SEPPELT

MADDIE

OBSESSION: PETER'S CROCS
FAVOURITE TOY: PETER'S CROCS
FAVOURITE FOOD: MARROWBONE
OWNERS: PETER AND ROZ SEPPELT
NAUGHTIEST DEED: STEALING PETER'S CROCS
FAVOURITE PASTIME: SLEEPING ON MELINDA'S BED

BUDDY

OBSESSION: STEVE
FAVOURITE TOY: STEVE
OWNER: IMOGEN LANGHAM
FAVOURITE PASTIME: CHASING
(AND CATCHING) HER OWN TAIL
PET HATE: SUDDEN MOVEMENTS
FAVOURITE FOOD: CHICKEN NECKS
NAUGHTIEST DEED: CHEWING THROUGH THE PRINTER CABLE

FAVOURITE FOOD: ICE CREAM
PET HATES: CROWS AND COWS
FAVOURITE TOY: SQUEAKY PIGGY
OBSESSIONS: FOOD AND SWIMMING
NAUGHTIEST DEED: DIGGING GIANT HOLES
UNDER PARKED CARS ON THE FARM
OWNERS: KERI GRAHAM AND ANTHONY LUTT
FAVOURITE PASTIME: GETTING PATS AT CELLAR DOOR

SKYLA

PET HATES: PELICANS AND SEAGULLS
FAVOURITE FOOD: SLOW-COOKED
LAMB SHANKS WITH MASHED POTATO
OWNERS: TRAVIS AND ELIZABETH WRAY
FAVOURITE PASTIME: ANYTHING BEACH-RELATED
NAUGHTIEST DEED: EATING ALL THE BUILDERS' LUNCHES
WHILE THEY WERE WORKING ON THE DECK AT CELLAR DOOR
OBSESSION: CHASING PELICANS AND SEAGULLS AT THE BEACH

MONTY

OTIS

OWNER: BEV COWLEY
FAVOURITE TOY: BALLS
OBSESSION: ANYTHING HI-VIZ
FAVOURITE FOODS: PIG'S EARS AND CHICKEN
PET HATES: BEING COLD AND GETTING UP EARLY
FAVOURITE PASTIME: GREETING CELLAR DOOR VISITORS
NAUGHTIEST DEED: HIDING IN THE WINE TOUR BUSES WITH VISITORS

TRUFFLE

OBSESSION: CHASING LEAVES
OWNERS: ROSLYN AND ERL HAPP
PET HATE: SWIMMING IN THE OCEAN
FAVOURITE PASTIME: PLAYING WITH KIDS
FAVOURITE TOY: TOY FROG (NOW DEMOLISHED)
NAUGHTIEST DEEDS: SCROUNGING FOR TRUFFLES BEHIND
CELLAR DOOR AND COUNTER-SURFING FOR CHEESE
FAVOURITE FOODS: FRESHLY COOKED CHICKEN, RICE AND VEGIES

OWNER: CHLOÉ SIMON
OBSESSIONS: STICKS AND BALLS
FAVOURITE PASTIME: GOING TO THE BEACH
FAVOURITE TOY: ANYTHING THAT CAN BE THROWN
KNOWN ACCOMPLICE: ANYONE WHO WILL THROW A BALL
PET HATE: ANOTHER DOG GETTING TOO CLOSE TO HER STICK

NYAH

OBSESSION: *LICKING DISHES*
OWNERS: *MAX AND WILL DUFFY*
FAVOURITE TOYS: *FLUFFY MOUSE AND THE MOOSE MAT*
NAUGHTIEST DEED: *PLAYING IN THE MUD AFTER BATHING*
FAVOURITE PASTIME: *SLEEPING ON THE MOOSE MAT AT CELLAR DOOR*
PET HATE: *BEING DRAGGED BY THE TAIL BY HER CANINE SISTER BELLA*

OWNER: JOE CORY
FAVOURITE TOY: BUNGS
NAUGHTIEST DEED: HOARDING
STINKY SOCKS IN JOE'S BED
FAVOURITE FOOD: MEAT BONES
MATURED TO PERFECTION IN THE
WORLD-FAMOUS TERRA ROSSA SOIL
FAVOURITE PASTIMES: STALKING BIRDS
AND WATCHING 'DOWNTON ABBEY'
PET HATE: MAGPIES STEALING HIS FOOD

NEVILLE

MR BEAR

OBSESSION: FOOD
OWNERS: CHRIS AND JO DAVIES
FAVOURITE PASTIMES: SNOOZING IN THE
SUNSHINE AND PLAYING CHESS WITH PABLO
PET HATES: LOUD NOISES AND CHECKMATE
FAVOURITE TOY: ANYTHING THAT SQUEAKS
NAUGHTIEST DEED: HANGING OUT AT THE
CHOCOLATE FACTORY, PRETENDING TO BE STARVING

FAVOURITE FOOD: BONES
OBSESSION: CHASING RABBITS
PET HATE: MISSING OUT ON FUN
OWNERS: TIM AND SARAH DAVIES
NAUGHTIEST DEED: CHEWING BEDS
FAVOURITE PASTIME: CHEWING STICKS

PABLO

OWNER: MICHAEL KERRIGAN
FAVOURITE TOYS: ROCKS AND SOCKS
NAUGHTIEST DEED: SNATCHING A WHOLE
RAW CHICKEN FROM THE KITCHEN BENCH
FAVOURITE PASTIME: HELPING WITH VINTAGE
BY PRODUCT-TESTING BLOCK 2 CABERNET
OBSESSION: FOLLOWING MICHAEL EVERYWHERE
PET HATE: MICHAEL PACKING FOR OVERSEAS TRAVEL
KNOWN ACCOMPLICE: BONO THE GOLDEN RETRIEVER
FROM RUSTICO AT HAY SHED HILL RESTAURANT
FAVOURITE FOOD: ANYTHING DROPPED FROM A HIGHCHAIR

BECKY

OWNER: MARK COSTER
PET HATE: VACUUM CLEANERS
OBSESSIONS: PEOPLE AND PATS
FAVOURITE PASTIMES: EATING, SLEEPING
AND GETTING PATS AT CELLAR DOOR
NAUGHTIEST DEED: TIPPING OVER BEERS
AT PARTIES AND THEN DRINKING THEM
FAVOURITE TOYS: HER SOFT TOY AND PILLOW
FAVOURITE FOOD: FROZEN FRUITS IN SUMMERTIME

BACI

BELLA

OBSESSION: FOOD
PET HATES: THUNDER AND GUNSHOTS
OWNERS: IAN McKENZIE AND SUE CUTLER
NAUGHTIEST DEED: CHEWING SHOES AND SOCKS
FAVOURITE FOOD: ANYTHING EXCEPT GREEN PEAS
FAVOURITE TOYS: SHOES AND SOCKS (WHEN YOUNGER)
FAVOURITE PASTIME: CHASING VIRTUAL RABBITS IN HER SLEEP

OWNER: ALLAN SMITH
OBSESSION: HER OWNER
FAVOURITE FOOD: SCHMACKOS
FAVOURITE PASTIME: BEING AT WORK
NAUGHTIEST DEED: CHASING CYCLISTS
PET HATE: WEEKENDS AWAY FROM WORK
FAVOURITE TOY: SMELLY (A STUFFED TOY)

JAZZ

ASTA

FAVOURITE TOY: KES, HIS CAT
NAUGHTIEST DEED: ROUNDING UP ALL THE PENNY'S
HILL SHEEP THEN LETTING THEM BEAT HIM UP
OBSESSIONS: BABIES AND KITTENS (LOVES THEM)
FAVOURITE PASTIME: JUMPING UP ON THE COUNTER
TO SAY HELLO TO CUSTOMERS AT CELLAR DOOR
OWNERS: DAVID PARKINSON AND SYBIL LEBOIS-PARKINSON
FAVOURITE FOOD: BACON-WRAPPED CHEESE FROM AUNTY SONYA

PET HATE: BEING LEFT ALONE
OWNERS: FERDINANDO AND JOANNE DEBLASIO
FAVOURITE TOY: HIS TEDDY THAT HE HAS HAD SINCE HE WAS A PUP
FAVOURITE FOODS: SPAGHETTI BOLOGNESE AND HOMEMADE BREAD
NAUGHTIEST DEED: TRYING TO COME INSIDE WHEN HE SPOTS AN OPEN DOOR
OBSESSION: SHOWING HIS AFFECTION BY LICKING YOU WITH HIS SUPER-SIZED TONGUE
FAVOURITE PASTIMES: FOLLOWING HIS OWNERS AROUND THE VINEYARD AND SLEEPING

MASSIMO

From left:

MYA FAVOURITE PASTIME: ANNOYING DALMATIANS
OBSESSION: THE CAT'S FOOD
FAVOURITE FOOD: THE CAT'S FOOD
OWNERS: CHARLIE AND VIRGINIA MELTON
PET HATE: BEING LEFT OUT OF THE UTE RIDE

AXEL OBSESSION: CATS
FAVOURITE PASTIME: EXERCISE (LIFTING HIS HEAD
AND TAIL IN UNISON WHILE LAYING ON HIS SIDE)
PET HATE: ANDREW LLOYD WEBBER
AND THAT BLOODY MUSICAL
NAUGHTIEST DEED: CHASING CATS
OWNERS: CHARLIE AND VIRGINIA MELTON

MAJOR PET HATE: DOORS
OWNERS: CHARLIE AND VIRGINIA MELTON
FAVOURITE PASTIMES: FARTING AND RUNNING
NAUGHTIEST DEED: CAUSING MORTAL DAMAGE TO
BUCKY, THE GREATEST MAGPIE THAT EVER LIVED

EDEA

PET HATE: HOSES
FAVOURITE FOOD: PIZZA
OWNER: MATT DUNNING
FAVOURITE TOY: FOOTBALL
NAUGHTIEST DEED: BARKING
FAVOURITE PASTIME: STALKING
OBSESSION: ANYTHING AIRBORNE

HANK

OBSESSION: BALLS
FAVOURITE FOOD: PIZZA
OWNER: MATT DUNNING
PET HATE: HOT AIR BALLOONS
FAVOURITE TOY: SIX STITCHER
NAUGHTIEST DEED: STEALING BUNGS
FAVOURITE PASTIME: PLAYING CRICKET

FRUIT DRIVEN.
THE NOSE IS PILLOWS,
SHEETS, BLANKETS.
IN THE MOUTH IT IS
SOFT AND WARM WITH
GOOD SUPPORT   A
NICELY SPRUNG WINE
WITH A SLOW FINISH

SLEEPY CREEK PINOT NOIR

FRUIT DRIVEN.

BREEZY AROMAS OF
DRY GRASS, GRANITE BOULDERS,
FENCE POSTS, MUSHROOMS and
THISTLES.
THE PALATE IS BROAD,
UNDULATING WITH SOME
LIGHT CLOUDS AT THE
FINISH — WITH A LONE
COW AND A RABBIT.

EMPTY PADDOCK CHARDONNAY

FRUIT DRIVEN.

WILD BUSTLING VAPORS
OF ROTTING KAPOK, OLD
BOOKS, MELTED LIPSTICK,
BURNT TOAST AND CAR
UPHOLSTERY. IN THE
MOUTH THERE IS THE SOFT
SLIPPERY SENSATION OF A
TONGUE WHICH IS POINTY
AT THE FINISH.

BLACK HOLE ESTATE LATE PICKED SHIRAZ

FRUIT DRIVEN
FRUIT DRIVEN
FRUIT DRIVEN
BANANAS, COCONUTS, PAW PAWS
PINEAPPLES, CHOCOLATE, MINT
TOFFEE, TOBACCO, KIT-KAT
MARS BARS, COFFEE,
PARKING FINES, LOVE
LETTERS...AND... UMM...

FRUIT DRIVEN !

WINE WRITER'S TUNNEL CLASSIC NOUVEAU '99

Leunig

179

BINGO

OBSESSION: RABBITS
FAVOURITE PASTIME: BEING CUDDLED
FAVOURITE FOOD: VINEYARD PLATTER
OWNERS: RICHARD AND ALICE MACDOUGALL
NAUGHTIEST DEED: BURYING A BONE IN GRANDMA'S GARDEN
KNOWN ACCOMPLICES: YOUNG GIRLS WHO LOVE TO PET AND CUDDLE HIM

OBSESSION: SOCKS
OWNER: KIRSTY DANIEL
PET HATE: GETTING INTO TROUBLE
FAVOURITE PASTIME: EXPLORING THE
SEPPELT UNDERGROUND CELLARS
FAVOURITE TOY: RUBBER SQUEAKY DUCK
NAUGHTIEST DEED: PULLING EVERY PLANT
OUT OF ITS POT, INCLUDING PRICKLY CACTUS

MORTICIA

JESS

OWNER: TIM McCARTHY
FAVOURITE TOY: THE KIDS
FAVOURITE FOOD: LAMB SHANKS
PET HATE: TIM GROWLING AT HER
NAUGHTIEST DEEDS: DIGGING UNDER THE
HOUSE AND DROPPING ROCKS ON THE LAWN
OBSESSION: ROUNDING UP EVERYTHING THAT MOVES
FAVOURITE PASTIME: ROLLING IN SHEEP AND COW MANURE

SARAN

OWNER: DIANE STRATTON
PET HATE: BEING TOLD OFF
FAVOURITE PASTIME: SLEEPING
NAUGHTIEST DEED: DECORATING
THE HOUSE WITH MUDDY PAW PRINTS
OBSESSION: GETTING OUT OF THE DOOR
AT THE SAME TIME AS THE OTHERS
FAVOURITE FOOD: ROAST VEGETABLES

PET HATE: DIETS
OWNER: DIANE STRATTON
FAVOURITE FOOD: MEATY BONES
FAVOURITE PASTIME: SUNBATHING
NAUGHTIEST DEED: COUNTER-SURFING
OBSESSION: GETTING OUT OF THE
DOOR AT THE SAME TIME AS THE OTHERS
FAVOURITE TOY: ANY TOY FILLED WITH FOOD TREATS

NIA

OWNER: DIANE STRATTON
FAVOURITE FOOD: ROAST CHICKEN
NAUGHTIEST DEED: CHEWING HOLES
IN ALL THE SOFA THROW RUGS
OBSESSION: GETTING OUT OF THE DOOR
AT THE SAME TIME AS THE OTHERS
FAVOURITE TOY: INVINCIBLE SQUEAKY SNAKE
PET HATE: GOING OUTSIDE WHEN IT'S RAINING
FAVOURITE PASTIME: CHASING THE OCCASIONAL KANGAROO

FAVOURITE FOOD: YOGHURT
OWNER: DIANE STRATTON
FAVOURITE TOY: CRINKLY ZEBRA
NAUGHTIEST DEED: TURNING LITTLE
HOLES IN THE LAWN INTO BIG HOLES
PET HATE: QUIET TIME IN HER CRATE
OBSESSION: GETTING OUT OF THE DOOR
AT THE SAME TIME AS THE OTHERS
FAVOURITE PASTIME: RUNNING ON THE BEACH

TIGER

RAYA

ANGAS

PET HATE: *PUPARAZZI*
OWNER: *HAMISH MAGUIRE*
FAVOURITE PASTIME: *CROSS-FIT*
FAVOURITE TOY: *SWISS ARMY KNIFE*
NAUGHTIEST DEED: *PARTYING ALL NIGHT, SLEEPING ALL DAY*
OBSESSIONS: *1920s AMERICAN JAZZ AND BORDER SECURITY*
FAVOURITE FOODS: *GREEN SMOOTHIES AND DUMPSTER DIVING*

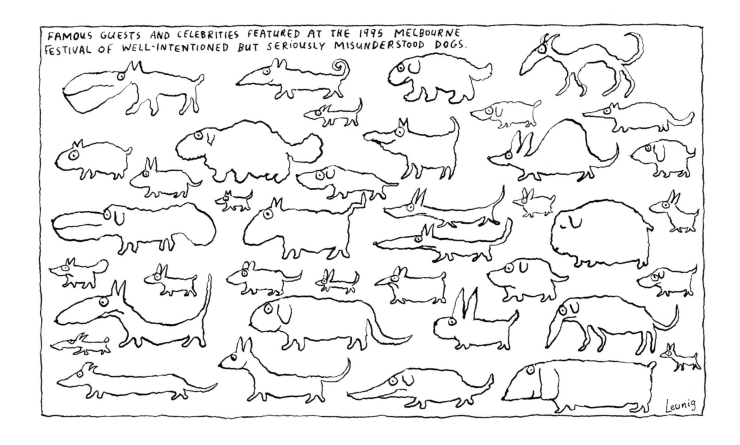

FAMOUS GUESTS AND CELEBRITIES FEATURED AT THE 1995 MELBOURNE FESTIVAL OF WELL-INTENTIONED BUT SERIOUSLY MISUNDERSTOOD DOGS.

Leunig

FAVOURITE FOOD: GRAVY
FAVOURITE TOY: A FLAT FOOTY
OWNERS: THE SISSINS FAMILY
FAVOURITE PASTIME: SLEEPING
OBSESSIONS: CATTLE AND FOOD
PET HATES: SALAD AND VEGETABLES
NAUGHTIEST DEED: HAVING SELECTIVE HEARING

ZAC

PHOTOGRAPHY

Craig with Tule Bollibakka from Silver Oak Cellars, Oakville CA USA

PHOTOGRAPHY © CRAIG MCGILL 2017

SUSAN ELLIOTT

PUBLISHER, DESIGNER

Susan is a multi-skilled artist with a background in fine art, illustration and printmaking. After completing two years of a psychology degree, Sue changed to a career in art. She graduated from The City Art Institute in 1986, majoring in drawing, printmaking and painting.

After two years living abroad, Sue returned to Australia and exhibited her graphic art and screenprints extensively around Sydney, while also working in a number of small design studios. She has developed into an award-winning graphic designer with over 20 years of experience in the industry.

Sue joined McGill Design Group in 1999 as co-owner and Creative Director. She is also co-founder and principal of the Giant Dog publishing house, which is responsible for producing a number of best-selling books, including the *Wine Dogs* titles. She recently designed five *Wine Dogs* stamps for Australia Post.

Sue's knowledge of dogs is unparalleled, and in the past she has also found time to be a successful Siberian Husky breeder. Although currently dogless, Sue loves to spend time with the many wine dogs she meets from around the world as well as a feisty cichlid named Ron.

CRAIG McGILL

PUBLISHER, PHOTOGRAPHER

Originally from Shepparton in Victoria, Australia, Craig is a self-taught designer and illustrator who started his own design business in Melbourne at 18 years of age. During that time he was appointed as a design consultant to The Reserve Bank of Australia.

His designs and illustrations have graced banknotes throughout the world, including the Australian bicentenary ten-dollar note. His work appears on the original Australian $100 note, Papua New Guinea Kina, Cook Islands Dollars and English Pound traveller's cheques. Craig was also involved in the design and illustration of many countries' security documents such as Passports, Bonds and Traveller's Cheques.

At the age of 23 he designed the entire series of the Cook Islands banknotes and it is believed that he was the world's youngest designer to design a country's

complete currency. In 1991, Craig moved to Sydney where his illustrations were regularly commissioned by agencies and designers both in Australia and around the world.

He is now widely known as Australia's only freelance currency designer. Craig has also designed and illustrated nine stamps for Australia Post. Five of his *Wine Dogs* photos have also been used on stamps for Australia Post.

Craig has been Creative Director of his own agency, McGill Design Group, for over twenty-five years.

Having grown up with a succession of beagles and huskies, Craig is currently road-testing several hundred dog breeds from wineries around the world. www.realnasty.com.au

GIANT DOG PUBLISHING

Giant Dog is a niche independent publishing house specialising in producing benchmark quality design and art books. Recent publications include *Wine Cats*, *Wine Dogs California*, *Wine Dogs Australia 5*, *Wine Dogs Italy*, *Wine Dogs New Zealand 2* and *Footy Dogs*. www.giantdog.com.au

McGILL DESIGN GROUP

McGill Design Group was formed in 1981 and specialises in providing a wide range of quality graphic design services. The studio has produced numerous fine wine labels and packaging as well as corporate identities, advertising, publications and television commercials. www.mcgilldesigngroup.com

WINERY and VINEYARD LISTINGS

NEW SOUTH WALES

Allandale Winery PAGE 22
132 Lovedale Road,
Lovedale NSW 2325
Ph: (02) 4990 4526
www.allandalewinery.com.au

Briar Ridge Vineyard PAGE 149
593 Mount View Road,
Mount View NSW 2325
Ph: (02) 4990 3670
www.briarridge.com.au

Brokenwood Wines PAGE 30
401 McDonalds Road,
Pokolbin NSW 2320
Ph: (02) 4998 7559
www.brokenwood.com.au

**De Bortoli Wines,
Riverina** PAGE 106
De Bortoli Road, Bilbul NSW 2680
Ph: (02) 6966 0100
www.debortoli.com.au

Domaine de Binet PAGE 53
469 Lovedale Road,
Lovedale NSW 2325
Ph: 0421 696 262
www.domainedebinet.com.au

Dryridge Estate PAGES 94, 95
226 Aspinall Road,
Megalong Valley NSW 2785
Ph: 0403 118 990
www.dryridge.com.au

Glandore Estate Wines PAGE 17
1595 Broke Road,
Pokolbin NSW 2320
Ph: (02) 4998 7140
www.glandorewines.com

James Estate Wines PAGE 118
1142 Hermitage Road,
Pokolbin NSW 2320
Ph: (02) 4998 7992
www.jamesestatewines.com.au

Keith Tulloch Wine PAGES 24, 25
989 Hermitage Road,
Pokolbin NSW 2320
Ph: (02) 4998 7500
www.keithtullochwine.com.au

Lakes Folly PAGE 26
2416 Broke Road,
Pokolbin NSW 2320
Ph: (02) 4998 7507
www.lakesfolly.wine

Marsh Estate PAGE 113
95 Deasys Road,
Pokolbin NSW 2320
Ph: (02) 4998 7587
www.marshestate.com.au

Moorebank Vineyard PAGE 69
150 Palmers Lane,
Pokolbin NSW 2320
Ph: (02) 4998 7610
www.moorebankvineyard.com.au

Murrumbateman Winery PAGE 143
131 McIntosh Circuit,
Murrumbateman NSW 2582
Ph: 0432 826 454
www.murrumbatemanwinery.com.au

Oakvale Wines PAGE 76
1595 Broke Road,
Pokolbin NSW 2320
Ph: (02) 4998 7088
www.oakvalewines.com.au

Pepper Tree Wines PAGE 149
86 Halls Road,
Pokolbin NSW 2320
Ph: (02) 4909 7100
www.peppertreewines.com.au

Piggs Peake Winery PAGE 154
697 Hermitage Road,
Pokolbin NSW 2320
Ph: (02) 6574 7000
www.piggspeake.com

Pokolbin Estate Vineyard PAGE 126
298 McDonalds Road,
Pokolbin NSW 2320
Ph: (02) 4998 7524
www.pokolbinestate.com.au

Tyrrell's Wines PAGE 65
1838 Broke Road,
Pokolbin NSW 2320
Ph: (02) 4993 7000
www.tyrrells.com.au

Tinklers Wines PAGE 121
53 Pokolbin Mountains Road,
Pokolbin NSW 2320
Ph: (02) 4998 7435
www.tinklers.com.au

Tintilla Estate PAGE 130
725 Hermitage Road,
Pokolbin NSW 2320
Ph: (02) 6574 7093
www.tintilla.com.au

SOUTH AUSTRALIA

Artwine PAGES 6, 40
72 Bird-in-Hand Road,
Woodside SA 5244
Ph: (08) 8389 9399
www.artwine.com.au

Barossa Chateau PAGE 14
35 Hermann Thumm Drive,
Lyndoch SA 5351
Ph: (08) 8524 4920
www.barossachateau.com

Battle of Bosworth PAGES 70, 71
92 Gaffney Road,
Willunga SA 5172
Ph: (08) 8556 2441
www.battleofbosworth.com.au

Beach Road Wines PAGE 85
309 Seaview Road,
McLaren Vale SA 5171
Ph: (08) 8323 7344
www.beachroadwines.com.au

Burge Family Winemakers PAGE 87
1312 Barossa Valley Way,
Lyndoch SA 5351
Ph: (08) 8524 4644
www.burgefamily.com.au

Cape Jaffa Wines PAGES 88, 89
459 Limestone Coast Road,
Mt Benson SA 5276
Ph: (08) 8768 5053
www.capejaffawines.com.au

Charles Melton Wines
PAGES 176, 177
Krondorf Road, Krondorf SA 5352
Ph: (08) 8563 3606
www.charlesmeltonwines.com.au

Chateau Yaldara PAGE 173
159 Hermann Thumm Drive,
Lyndoch SA 5351
Ph: (08) 8524 0225
www.chateauyaldara.com.au

d'Arenberg PAGES 34, 35
Osborn Road, McLaren Vale SA 5171
Ph: (08) 8329 4888
www.darenberg.com.au

DogRidge PAGE 102
129 Bagshaws Road,
McLaren Flat SA 5171
Ph: (08) 8383 0140
www.dogridge.com.au

Flaxman Wines PAGE 133
662 Flaxmans Valley Road,
Flaxman Valley SA 5353
Ph: 0411 668 949
www.flaxmanwines.com.au

Gibson Wines PAGE 19
190 Willows Road,
Light Pass SA 5355
Ph: (08) 8562 4224
www.gibsonwines.com.au

Golding Wines PAGE 162
52 Western Branch Road,
Lobethal SA 5241
Ph: (08) 8389 5120
www.goldingwines.com.au

Graham Stevens Wines PAGE 164
72 Ingoldby Road,
McLaren Flat SA 5171
Ph: (08) 8383 0997
www.grahamstevenswines.com.au

Henschke Cellars PAGE 16
1428 Keyneton Road,
Keyneton SA 5353
Ph: (08) 8564 8223
www.henschke.com.au

Hewitson Winery PAGES 184, 185
1/66 Seppeltsfield Road,
Nuriootpa SA 5355
Ph: (08) 8212 6233
www.hewitson.com.au

Hollick Estates PAGE 167
1 Ravenswood Lane,
Coonawarra SA 5263
Ph: (08) 8737 2318
www.hollick.com

Hugh Hamilton Wines PAGE 10
94 McMurtrie Road,
McLaren Vale SA 5171
Ph: (08) 8323 8689
www.hughhamiltonwines.com.au

Jacob's Creek Wines PAGE 80
2129 Barossa Valley Way,
Rowland Flat SA 5352
Ph: (08) 8521 3000
www.jacobscreek.com

Jim Barry Wines PAGE 136
33 Craig Hill Road,
Clare SA 5453
Ph: (08) 8842 2261
www.jimbarry.com

K1 by Geoff Hardy PAGE 161
159 Tynan Road,
Kuitpo SA 5172
Ph: (08) 8388 3700
www.winesbygeoffhardy.com.au

Kaesler Wines PAGE 166
Barossa Valley Way,
Nuriootpa SA 5355
Ph: (08) 8562 4488
www.kaesler.com.au

Katnook Estate PAGE 112
15310 Riddoch Highway,
Penola SA 5277
Ph: (08) 8737 0300
www.katnookestate.com.au

Kies Family Wines PAGE 103
Lot 2, Barossa Valley Way,
Lyndoch SA 5351
Ph: (08) 8524 4110
www.kieswines.com.au

Lambert Estate Wines PAGE 183
55 Long Gully Road,
Angaston SA 5353
Ph: (08) 8564 2222
www.lambertestate.com

Lindsay Wine Estate PAGE 178
15 Vine Vale Road, Tanunda SA 5352
Ph: (08) 8563 3858
www.lindsaywineestate.com.au

Maxwell Wines PAGES 56, 57
19 Olivers Road,
McLaren Vale SA 5171
Ph: (08) 8323 8200
www.maxwellwines.com.au

Mitchell Wines PAGE 141
246 Hughes Park Road,
Sevenhill SA 5453
Ph: (08) 8843 4258
www.mitchellwines.com

Mt Lofty Ranges Vineyard PAGE 55
166 Harris Road,
Lenswood SA 5240
Ph: (08) 8389 8339
www.mtloftyrangesvineyard.com.au

O'Leary Walker Wines PAGE 96
7093 Horrocks Highway,
Leasingham SA 5452
Ph: (08) 8843 0022
www.olearywalkerwines.com

Oliver's Taranga Vineyards PAGE 111
246 Seaview Road,
McLaren Vale SA 5171
Ph: (08) 8323 8498
www.oliverstaranga.com

Penley Estate PAGES 28, 29
McLeans Road,
Coonawarra SA 5263
Ph: (08) 8736 3211
www.penley.com.au

Penny's Hill PAGE 174
281 Main Road,
McLaren Vale SA 5171
Ph: (08) 8557 0800
www.pennyshill.com.au

Peter Lehmann Wines PAGE 21
Para Road, Tanunda SA 5352
Ph: (08) 8565 9500
www.peterlehmannwines.com

Peter Seppelt Wines,
Grand Cru Estate PAGE 153
Lot 274, Laubes Road,
Springton SA 5235
Ph: (08) 8568 2452
www.peterseppeltwines.com.au

Ralph Fowler Wines PAGE 138
498 Limestone Coast Road,
Wangolina, Kingston SE, SA 5275
Ph: (08) 8768 5000
www.ralphfowlerwines.com

Reilly's Wines PAGE 140
Cnr Leasingham Road
and Hill Street,
Mintaro SA 5415
Ph: (08) 8843 9013
www.reillyswines.com.au

Rymill Coonawarra PAGE 38
Riddoch Highway,
Coonawarra SA 5263
Ph: (08) 8736 5001
www.rymill.com.au

S.C. Pannell Wines PAGE 129
60 Olivers Road,
McLaren Vale SA 5171
Ph: (08) 8323 8000
www.pannell.com.au

SOUTH AUSTRALIA *continued*

Saltram Wine Estates
PAGE 39
Angaston Road,
Angaston SA 5353
Ph: (08) 8561 0200
www.saltramwines.com.au

Seppeltsfield Wines PAGE 132
Seppeltsfield Road,
Seppeltsfield SA 5355
Ph: (08) 8568 6200
www.seppeltsfield.com.au

Shottesbrooke PAGE 186
101 Bagshaws Road,
McLaren Flat SA 5171
Ph: (08) 8383 0002
www.shottesbrooke.com.au

St Hugo Wines PAGE 182
2141 Barossa Valley Way,
Rowland Flat SA 5352
Ph: (08) 8115 9200
www.sthugo.com

The Blok Estate
Coonawarra PAGE 120
15535 Riddoch Highway,
Coonawarra SA 5263
Ph: (08) 8737 2734
www.blok.com.au

The Lane Vineyard PAGE 81
5 Ravenswood Lane,
Hahndorf SA 5245
Ph: (08) 8388 1250
www.thelane.com.au

Torbreck PAGE 116
348 Roennfeldt Road,
Marananga SA 5355
Ph: (08) 8562 4155
www.torbreck.com

Two Hands Wines PAGE 20
273 Neldner Road,
Marananga SA 5355
Ph: (08) 8562 4566
www.twohandswines.com

Wangolina PAGES 44, 45
8 Limestone Coast Road,
Wangolina SA 5275
Ph: (08) 8768 6187
www.wangolina.com.au

Whistler Wines PAGE 99
241 Seppeltsfield Road,
Marananga SA 5355
Ph: (08) 8562 4942
www.whistlerwines.com

Wirra Wirra Vineyards PAGE 119
McMurtrie Road,
McLaren Vale SA 5171
Ph: (08) 8323 8414
www.wirrawirra.com.au

TASMANIA

Delamere Vineyards PAGES 74, 75
4238 Bridport Road,
Pipers Brook TAS 7254
Ph: (03) 6382 7190
www.delamerevineyards.com.au

Every Man and His Dog
Vineyard PAGE 15
1314 Richmond Road,
Richmond TAS 7025
Ph: 0417 664 634
www.everymanandhisdog
vineyard.com

Frogmore Creek Wines PAGE 134
20 Denholms Road,
Cambridge TAS 7170
Ph: (03) 6248 5844
www.frogmorecreek.com.au

Holm Oak Vineyards PAGE 160
1 West Bay Road,
Rowella TAS 7270
Ph: (03) 6394 7577
www.holmoakvineyards.com.au

Moores Hill PAGE 148
3343 West Tamar Highway,
Sidmouth TAS 7270
Ph: (03) 6394 7649
www.mooreshill.com.au

Pipers Brook Vineyard PAGE 125
1216 Pipers Brook Road,
Pipers Brook TAS 7254
Ph: (03) 6382 7555
www.pipersbrook.com

Pooley Wines PAGE 98
1431 Richmond Road,
Richmond TAS 7025
Ph: (03) 6260 2895
www.pooleywines.com.au

Puddleduck Vineyard PAGE 128
992 Richmond Road,
Richmond TAS 7025
Ph: (03) 6260 2301
www.puddleduck.com.au

Stefano Lubiana Wines PAGE 83
60 Rowbottoms Road,
Granton TAS 7030
Ph: (03) 6263 7457
www.slw.com.au

Swinging Gate Vineyard PAGE 82
103 Glendale Road,
Sidmouth TAS 7270
Ph: 0419 599 710
www.swinginggatewines.com.au

Wobbly Boot Vineyard PAGE 122
487 White Kangaroo Road,
Campania TAS 7026
Ph: 0427 679 096
www.wobblybootvineyard.com.au

VICTORIA

All Saints Estate PAGES 12, 13
315 All Saints Road,
Wahgunyah VIC 3687
Ph: (02) 6035 2222
www.allsaintswine.com.au

Andrew Buller Wines PAGE 86
352 Jacks Road, Rutherglen VIC 3685
Ph: (02) 6032 9487
www.andrewbullerwines.com.au

Bannockburn Vineyards PAGE 23
94 Kelly Lane,
Bannockburn VIC 3331
Ph: (03) 5281 1363
www.bannockburnvineyards.com

Bellbrae Estate PAGE 180
520 Great Ocean Road,
Bellbrae VIC 3228
Ph: (03) 5264 8480
www.bellbraeestate.com.au

Billy Button Wines PAGE 72
11 Camp Street, Bright VIC 3741
Ph: (03) 5755 1569
www.billybuttonwines.com.au

Blackjack WInery PAGE 172
3379 Harmony Way,
Harcourt VIC 3453
Ph: (03) 5474 2355
www.blackjackwines.com.au

Brown Brothers PAGE 147
239 Milawa-Bobinawarrah Road,
Milawa VIC 3678
Ph: (03) 5720 5500
www.brownbrothers.com.au

**Chambers Rosewood
Winery** PAGE 90
Barkly Street, Rutherglen VIC 3685
Ph: (02) 6032 8641
www.chambersrosewood.com.au

Chandon PAGES 92, 93
727 Maroondah Highway,
Coldstream VIC 3770
Ph: (03) 9738 9200
www.chandon.com.au

**Clyde Park Vineyard
and Bistro** PAGE 48
2490 Midland Highway,
Bannockburn VIC 3331
Ph: (03) 5281 7274
www.clydepark.com.au

Crittenden Estate PAGES 50, 51
25 Harrisons Road,
Dromana VIC 3936
Ph: (03) 5987 3800
www.crittendenwines.com.au

Dal Zotto Wines PAGES 104, 105
4861 Wangaratta-Whitfield Road,
Whitfield VIC 3733
Ph: (03) 5729 8321
www.dalzotto.com.au

**De Bortoli Wines,
Yarra Valley** PAGE 107
58 Pinnacle Lane,
Dixons Creek VIC 3775
Ph: (03) 5965 2271
www.debortoli.com.au

Flynns Wines PAGE 135
29 Lewis Road, Heathcote VIC 3523
Ph: (03) 5433 6297
www.flynnswines.com

Grampians Estate PAGE 163
1477 Western Highway,
Great Western VIC 3374
Ph: (03) 5356 2400
www.grampiansestate.com.au

Greenstone Vineyards PAGES 100, 101
179 Glenview Road,
Yarra Glen VIC 3775
Ph: (03) 9730 1022
www.greenstonevineyards.com.au

Hanrahan Estate PAGE 156
3 Hexham Road, Gruyere VIC 3770
Ph: 0421 340 810
www.hanrahan.com.au

Jones Winery and Vineyard PAGE 18
61 Jones Road, Rutherglen VIC 3685
Ph: (02) 6032 8496
www.joneswinery.com

Levantine Hill Estate PAGES 66–68
882 Maroondah Highway,
Coldstream VIC 3770
Ph: (03) 5962 1333
www.levantinehill.com.au

Main Ridge Estate PAGE 144
80 William Road, Red Hill VIC 3937
Ph: (03) 5989 2686
www.mre.com.au

Montalto Vineyard PAGE 27
33 Red Hill-Shoreham Road,
Red Hill VIC 3937
Ph: (03) 5989 8412
www.montalto.com.au

Mount Langi Ghiran PAGES 150, 151
80 Vine Road, Bayindeen VIC 3375
Ph: (03) 5354 3207
www.langi.com.au

Oak Valley Estate PAGE 175
3055 Deakin Avenue,
Mildura VIC 3500
Ph: (03) 5021 2379
www.oakvalleyestate.com.au

Rob Dolan Wines PAGE 152
21–23 Delaneys Road,
South Warrandyte,
Yarra Valley VIC 3134
Ph: (03) 9876 5885
www.robdolanwines.com.au

Rowsley Fault Vineyards PAGE 137
131 Lumbs Road,
Sutherlands Creek VIC 3331
Ph: (03) 5281 1811
www.rowsleyfaultwines.com

Sam Miranda Wines PAGE 110
1019 Snow Road, Oxley VIC 3678
Ph: (03) 5727 3888
www.sammiranda.com.au

Seppelt Wines PAGE 181
36 Cemetery Road Road,
Great Western VIC 3377
Ph: (03) 5361 2239
www.seppelt.com.au

Simão and Co. Wines PAGE 131
PO Box 231, Rutherglen VIC 3685
Ph: 0439 459 183
www.simaoandco.com.au

Stanton and Killeen Wines PAGE 142
440 Jacks Road,
Rutherglen VIC 3685
Ph: (02) 6032 9457
www.stantonandkilleenwines.com.au

Sutton Grange Winery PAGE 41
Carnochans Road,
Sutton Grange VIC 3448
Ph: (03) 8672 1478
www.suttongrange.com.au

Tahbilk PAGES 78, 79
254 O'Neils Road,
Tabilk VIC 3608
Ph: (03) 5794 2555
www.tahbilk.com.au

Tarrawarra Estate PAGES 188, 189
311 Healesville-Yarra Glen Road,
Yarra Glen VIC 3775
Ph: (03) 5957 3510
www.tarrawarra.com.au

Tokar Estate PAGE 84
6 Maddens Lane,
Coldstream VIC 3770
Ph: (03) 5964 9585
www.tokarestate.com.au

Warrabilla Wines PAGES 42, 43
6152 Murray Valley Highway,
Rutherglen VIC 3685
Ph: (02) 6035 7242
www.warrabillawines.com.au

WESTERN AUSTRALIA

Alkoomi Wines PAGE 77
1141 Wingebellup Road,
Frankland River WA 6396
Ph: (08) 9855 2229
www.alkoomiwines.com.au

Amelia Park Wines PAGE 11
3857 Caves Road,
Wilyabrup WA 6280
Ph: (08) 9755 6747
www.ameliaparkwines.com.au

Cape Grace Wines PAGE 59
281 Fifty One Road,
Cowaramup WA 6284
Ph: (08) 9755 5669
www.capegracewines.com.au

Cape Naturaliste Vineyard PAGE 91
1 Coley Road, Yallingup WA 6282
Ph: (08) 9755 2538
www.capenaturalistevineyard.com.au

Credaro Family Estate PAGES 32, 33
2715 Caves Road,
Yallingup WA 6282
Ph: (08) 9756 6520
wwwcredarowines.com.au

Cullen Wines PAGE 52
4323 Caves Road,
Wilyabrup WA 6280
Ph: (08) 9755 5277
www.cullenwines.com.au

estate 807 PAGE 146
807 Scotsdale Road,
Denmark WA 6333
Ph: (08) 9840 9027
www.estate807.com.au

Evans & Tate PAGES 170, 171
929 Metricup Road,
Willyabrup WA 6280
Ph: (08) 9755 6244
www.evansandtate.com.au

Fermoy Estate PAGE 123
838 Metricup Road,
Wilyabrup WA 6280
Ph: (08) 9755 6285
www.fermoy.com.au

Flametree Wines PAGE 54
7 Chain Avenue,
Dunsborough WA 6281
Ph: (08) 9756 8577
www.flametreewines.com

Happs Wines PAGES 158, 159
575 Commonage Road,
Quindalup WA 6281
Ph: (08) 9755 3300
www.happs.com.au

Harewood Estate PAGES 36, 37
1570 Scotsdale Road,
Denmark WA 6333
Ph: (08) 9840 9078
www.harewood.com.au

Hay Shed Hill Wines PAGE 169
511 Harmans Mill Road,
Willyabrup WA 6280
Ph: (08) 9755 6046
www.hayshedhill.com.au

House of Cards PAGE 155
4 Quininup Road,
Yallingup WA 6282
Ph: (08) 9755 2583
www.houseofcardswine.com.au

Howard Park Wines PAGE 108
543 Miamup Road,
Cowaramup WA 6284
Ph: (08) 9756 5200
www.howardparkwines.com.au

Leeuwin Estate PAGES 114, 115
Stevens Road,
Margaret River WA 6285
Ph: (08) 9759 0000
www.leeuwinestate.com.au

LS Merchants PAGE 58
PO Box 538, Cowaramup WA 6284
Ph: 0420 307 665
www.lsmerchants.com.au

Mandoon Estate PAGE 145
10 Harris Road,
Caversham WA 6055
Ph: (08) 6279 0500
www.mandoonestate.com.au

Plantagenet Wines PAGE 124
45 Albany Highway,
Mount Barker WA 6324
Ph: (08) 9851 3132
www.plantagenetwines.com

Stella Bella PAGES 60, 61
205 Rosa Brook Road,
Margaret River WA 6285
Ph: (08) 9758 8611
www.stellabella.com.au

Swings & Roundabouts
PAGES 62, 63
2807 Caves Road,
Yallingup WA 6281
Ph: (08) 9756 6640
www.swings.com.au

Voyager Estate PAGE 64
41 Stevens Road,
Margaret River WA 6285
Ph: (08) 9757 6354
www.voyagerestate.com.au

Wills Domain PAGES 46, 47
Lot 341, Brash Road,
Yallingup WA 6282
Ph: (08) 9755 2327
www.willsdomain.com.au

Windows Estate PAGE 168
4 Quininup Road,
Yallingup WA 6282
Ph: (08) 9756 6655
www.windowsestate.com

WINE DOGS BREED INDEX

WINE DOGS
California

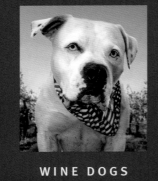

WINE DOGS

USA EDITION

the dogs of North American wineries

MᶜGILL • ELLIOTT

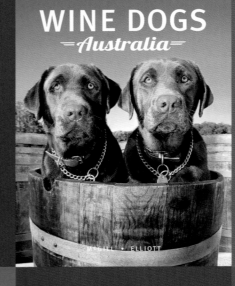

WINE DOGS
Australia

MᶜGILL • ELLIOTT

I CANI DEL VINO

WINE DOGS ITALY

i cani delle aziende vinicole Italiane

MᶜGILL • ELLIOTT

WINE DOGS

NEW ZEALAND

the dogs of New Zealand wineries

MᶜGILL • ELLIOTT • JUDD

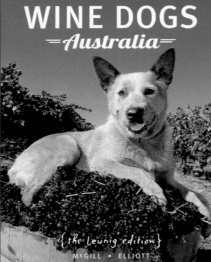

WINE DOGS
Australia

{the Leunig edition}

MᶜGILL • ELLIOTT

WINE DOGS USA

2

more dogs from North American wineries

MᶜGILL • ELLIOTT

WINE DOGS

AUSTRALIA

more dogs from Australian wineries

MᶜGILL • ELLIOTT

WINE DOGS
California

WINE DOGS

DELUXE EDITION

the dogs of Australasian wineries

MᶜGILL • ELLIOTT

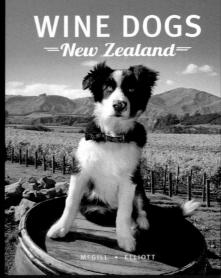

WINE DOGS
New Zealand

MᶜGILL • ELLIOTT

WINE DOGS

AUSTRALIA

3

more dogs from Australian wineries

MᶜGILL • ELLIOTT

WINE DOGS USA

3

more dogs from North American wineries

MᶜGILL • ELLIOTT

WINE CATS

MᶜGILL • ELLIOTT

WINE DOGS

AUSTRALIA

2

more dogs from Australian wineries

MᶜGILL • ELLIOTT

FOOTY DOGS

the dogs of Australian Rules football

MᶜGILL • ELLIOTT

WINE DOGS AUSTRALIA 5
ISBN 978-1-921336-56-0

COPYRIGHT © GIANT DOG, FIRST EDITION 2017
WINE DOGS® IS A REGISTERED TRADEMARK

DESIGNED BY SUSAN ELLIOTT, COPYRIGHT © McGILL DESIGN GROUP PTY LTD, 2017

ALL PHOTOGRAPHY © CRAIG McGILL, 2017
WITH THE EXCEPTION OF PAGE 181 © KIRSTY DANIEL AND PAGE 190 © SUSAN ELLIOTT
ENDPAPER ILLUSTRATIONS © CRAIG McGILL, 2017

ALL ILLUSTRATIONS © MICHAEL LEUNIG, 2017

EDITING AND PROOFREADING BY VICKY FISHER

PRINTED BY 1010 PRINTING INTERNATIONAL LIMITED, CHINA.

PUBLISHED BY GIANT DOG, ABN 27 110 894 178.
PO BOX 964, ROZELLE NSW 2039 AUSTRALIA
TELEPHONE: (+612) 9555 4077
WWW.WINEDOGS.COM

FOR ORDERS: ORDERS@WINEDOGS.COM

OPINIONS EXPRESSED IN WINE DOGS AUSTRALIA 5 ARE NOT NECESSARILY THOSE OF THE PUBLISHER.

OTHER TITLES BY CRAIG McGILL AND SUSAN ELLIOTT INCLUDE:
WINE DOGS: ORIGINAL EDITION – THE DOGS OF AUSTRALIAN WINERIES ISBN 0-9580856-1-7
WINE DOGS: DELUXE EDITION – THE DOGS OF AUSTRALASIAN WINERIES ISBN 0-9580856-2-5
FOOTY DOGS: THE DOGS OF AUSTRALIAN RULES FOOTBALL ISBN 0-9580856-3-3
WINE DOGS AUSTRALIA – MORE DOGS FROM AUSTRALIAN WINERIES ISBN 978-1-921336-02-7
WINE DOGS AUSTRALIA 2 – MORE DOGS FROM AUSTRALIAN WINERIES ISBN 978-1-921336-16-4
WINE DOGS AUSTRALIA 3 – MORE DOGS FROM AUSTRALIAN WINERIES ISBN 978-1-921336-28-7
WINE DOGS AUSTRALIA 4 ISBN 978-1-921336-48-5
WINE DOGS: USA EDITION – THE DOGS OF NORTH AMERICAN WINERIES ISBN 0-9580856-6-8
WINE DOGS USA 2 – MORE DOGS FROM NORTH AMERICAN WINERIES ISBN 978-1-921336-10-2
WINE DOGS USA 3 – MORE DOGS FROM NORTH AMERICAN WINERIES ISBN 978-1-921336-29-4
WINE DOGS CALIFORNIA ISBN 978-1-921336-43-0
WINE DOGS CALIFORNIA 2 ISBN 978-1-921336-50-8
WINE DOGS ITALY – THE DOGS OF ITALIAN WINERIES ISBN 978-1-921336-11-9
WINE DOGS NEW ZEALAND – THE DOGS OF NEW ZEALAND WINERIES ISBN 978-1-921336-12-6
WINE DOGS NEW ZEALAND 2 ISBN 978-1-921336-49-2
WINE CATS ISBN 978-1-921336-38-6

HEALTH WARNING: VETERINARY ASSOCIATIONS ADVISE THAT EATING GRAPES, SULTANAS OR RAISINS CAN
MAKE A DOG EXTREMELY ILL AND COULD POSSIBLY RESULT IN FATAL KIDNEY FAILURE. IN THE INTERESTS OF
CANINE HEALTH AND WELLBEING, DO NOT FEED YOUR DOG GRAPES OR ANY GRAPE BY-PRODUCT.

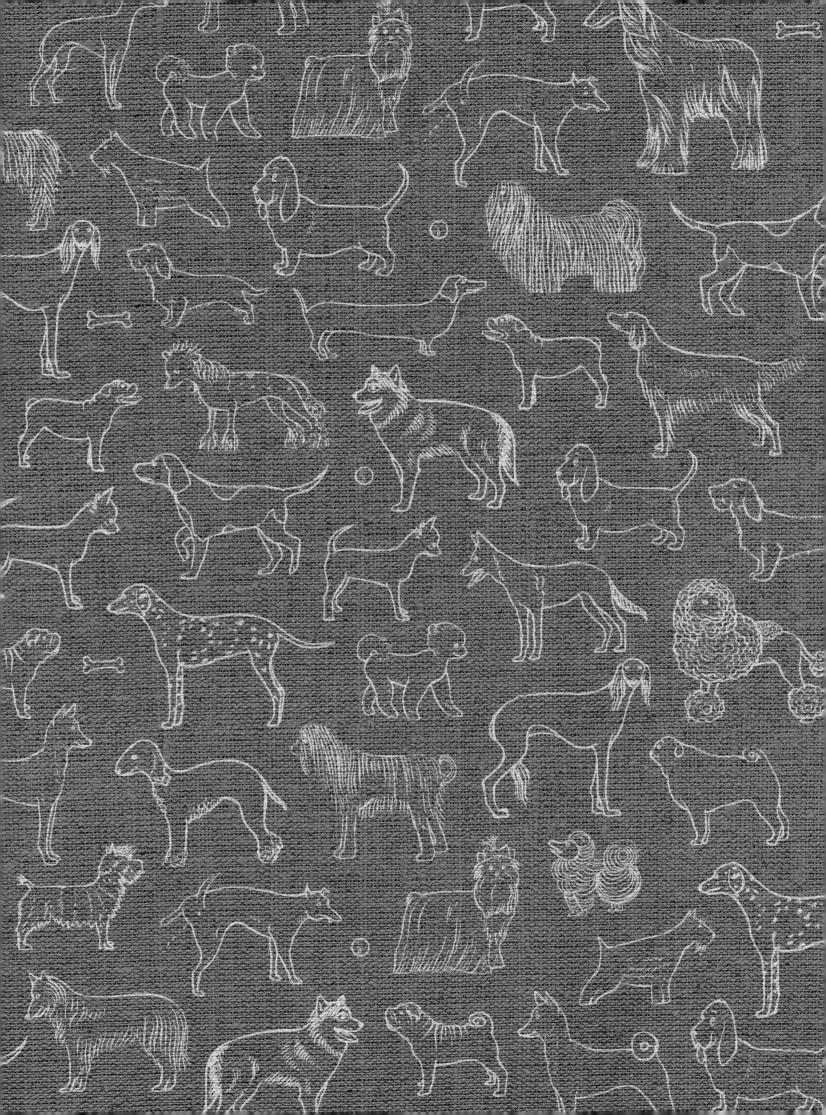

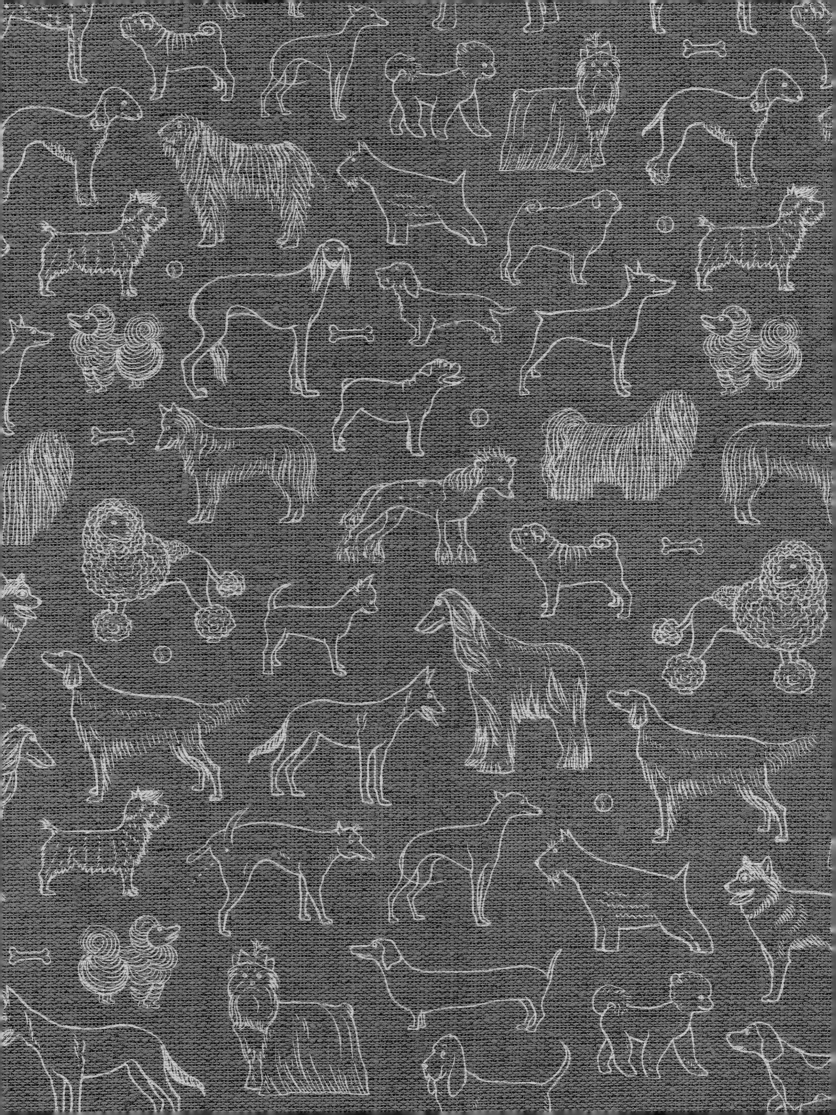